Y0-ARD-477

HOOVER INSTITUTION BIBLIOGRAPHICAL SERIES: XXVI

Stalin's Works

AN ANNOTATED BIBLIOGRAPHY

COMPILED BY

ROBERT H. McNEAL

THE HOOVER INSTITUTION ON WAR, REVOLUTION AND PEACE
STANFORD UNIVERSITY 1967

The Hoover Institution on War, Revolution and Peace, founded at Stanford University in 1919 by the late President Herbert Hoover, is a center for advanced study and research on public and international affairs in the twentieth century. The views expressed in its publications are entirely those of the authors and do not necessarily reflect the views of the Hoover Institution.

The Hoover Institution
on War, Revolution and Peace
Stanford, California
© 1967 by the Board of Trustees of the
Leland Stanford Junior University

Library of Congress Catalog Card Number: 67-15063
Printed in the United States of America

PREFACE

The mystery that surrounded Stalin during his lifetime is still difficult to fathom. For many, he remains a latter-day Genghis Khan, whereas there are those in the communist world who to this day consider the former Soviet dictator the guardian angel of the new utopia. There can be no denying, however, that Stalin is one of the major political figures in recent history. It was during his more than a quarter of a century reign that the U.S.S.R. developed into a first class world power. Stalin successfully obtained his objectives--victory over both domestic and foreign wartime enemies. Whether his success has outlived him is already in serious doubt, and this question is sure to be debated for years to come.

Perhaps equal in importance to Stalin's lifetime accomplishments is the posthumous use of his name as a symbol within the communist world. The degree of down- or upgrading of Stalin's place in the communist pantheon serves as a handy calibrator to measure divisions within the international communist movement and to indicate general shifts of policy within the individual communist countries.

This bibliography is intended as a serious scholarly tool to facilitate the study of Stalin's career. It starts with his earliest known published work--poems which appeared in 1895-96--and ends with a reference to the publication of Stalin's letter to James Reston in the December 26, 1952 issue of Pravda. In addition to the bibliographical listings, this work also contains substantial analytical essays by the compiler concerning the authenticity of material attributed to Stalin and the editorial policies followed by those who produced the official thirteen-volume Soviet collection of Stalin's works.

For the convenience of the researcher, this bibliography has been divided into two parts.

Part I covers Stalin's works from the beginning of his political career to early 1934--the same period contained within the original thirteen volumes mentioned above. It should be noted that the Soviet collection contains only 480 items, whereas 895 separate entries are listed here. The listing with extensive annotations of the omitted papers should prove most helpful to a wide variety of scholars and save them considerable time in their searchings.

Part II starts with 1934, the year when Stalinist totalitarianism is often considered to have started, and ends with December 1952, a few months before Stalin's death. For the coverage of this period--when Stalin's power was at its zenith--the compiler performs a substantial

service by listing only those items which can be truly attributed to
Stalin in any meaningful sense. An additional convenience for the schol
are the references made in this section to the location of many items
in the forthcoming I. V. Stalin – Sochineniia (Collected Works), soon to
be published by the Hoover Institution. This three-volume compendium
resumes the collection of Stalin's works starting with 1934--the last
date covered by the official Soviet collection--and includes Stalin's
papers to the time of his death in 1953.

Because of the importance of exploring Stalin's career to the
specialists in Russian history and communist affairs, the Hoover
Institution was fortunate to obtain the services of Dr. Robert H. McNea
who not only compiled this bibliography but also undertook the arduous
task of editing the abovementioned concluding volumes of Stalin's
collected works.

> K. Maichel, Curator
> East European Collection
> The Hoover Institution on War,
>   Revolution and Peace

ACKNOWLEDGEMENTS

This modest work must somehow bear a weighty burden of grati-
tude to the numerous persons and institutions who have so generously
helped it in diverse ways,

to Professor G. T. Robinson, who first encouraged me to
search beyond Stalin's Sochineniia for the leader's writings
and who first encouraged the conception of this bibliography,

to Professors Cyril E. Black, Alexander Dallin, and Philip E.
Mosely, who lent encouragement to the project,

to Messrs. R. Carter Elwood, Bertram D. Wolfe, and Professor André L. de Saint-Rat, who gave advice on some particular problems,

to Mr. Julian Laychuk, who was of invaluable assistance in
putting various material in order at an early stage of the
task,

to the Hoover Institution on War, Revolution, and Peace, and
especially to Messrs. Witold Sworakowski and Karol Maichel,
for undertaking the publication of the work and rendering
manifold assistance to that end,

to the University of Alberta for its major financial assistance
at the crucial stage of preparation of the bibliography and
to McMaster University for assistance near the end.

Robert H. McNeal

CONTENTS

THE FORMAT OF THE BIBLIOGRAPHY

Although the same basic format is used throughout both parts of this bibliography, the apparatus used in Part I, and especially the portion before 1917, includes certain features that are not needed in Part II. Basically, each entry consists of three possible sections: (1) heading (followed by translation into English, in square brackets); (2) place of original publication and comments (if any); and (3) location (if any) in Sochineniia. Dates are given in Old Style before February 1918.

A more detailed explanation of the procedures used in preparing each of these three sections follows:

Heading

For items that have an established Russian title, this is given, along with a parenthetical translation of the title in English and, when applicable, a parenthetical note that the Russian is actually a translation from Georgian. For items such as letters and speeches, which very often have no established title in Russian (simply "Letter to Lenin" or the like), only a heading in English is given. Such labels often include a date of origin. When available English translations of titles are taken from the English edition of Stalin's Works (Foreign Languages Publishing House).

Place of original publication and comments

The place of earliest known publication of each item is indicated, except for items first published in the Sochineniia, which are noted as such. Because so many items were republished on such a wide scale, no republications subsequent to the first known one are indicated. Whenever possible, the earliest known publication of a given item has been compared to the version of it in Vols. I-XIII of the Sochineniia. When such a comparison has been made, the earliest known publication is marked with an asterisk (*). Items for which the original publication could not be found are not marked in this way, nor is the mark used at all in Part II because there is no official Sochineniia covering this period. Questions of authenticity and the reliability of the Sochineniia version of a given document are noted; if the item did appear in the Sochineniia and there is no comment on alterations, one may assume that the Sochineniia version is in the main reliable. In the early years of Stalin's career, during which the question of authenticity is especially important, any information regarding signatures is given. From 1917 through 1933, however, there is no significant variation in Stalin's signatures, and the bibliography only indicates whether or not a given item was signed by him at all. No comment on signatures would be significant in Part II, since there is no doubt about the official attribution of his published writings in this period. When Stalin is a co-signatory of a given item, that is indicated; otherwise one may assume that he was the sole signatory.

Location in Sochineniia

Items that do appear in the Sochineniia are indicated simply by a volume number in Roman numerals and page number(s) in Arabic numerals (e.g., II, 124). To avoid redundancy, no other publication information is given for this work. When no such reference occurs following the title material, one may assume that the item does not appear in the Sochineniia. In Part II of the bibliography, references are to the Hoover Institution's unofficial completion of the official Soviet edition, since the latter does not cover February 1934 - March 1953. Although the volume and page numbers for the English translation of the Sochineniia are not provided, these are generally quite close to the pagination in the Russian edition.

LIST OF ABBREVIATIONS

Anisimov--N. Anisimov, "O bibliografii proizvedenii I. V. Stalina," Istorik Marksist, no. 1, 1940.

B--Bol'shevik

Beria--L. P. Beria, K voprosu ob istorii bol'shevistskikh organizatsii v zakavkaz'e (Moscow: Ogiz, 1938, 4th ed.).

Dokumenty...Petrograda--Dokumenty o geroicheskoi oborone Petrograda v 1919 g. (Moscow: Gos. izd. pol. lit., 1941).

Dokumenty...Tsaritsyna--Dokumenty o geroicheskoi oborone Tsaritsyna v 1918 g. (Moscow: Gospolitizdat, 1942).

Kniga i Proletarskaia Revoliutsiia--Gosudarstvennaia biblioteka imeni V. I. Lenina (M. K. Derunova et al.), "Bibliograficheskii ukazatel' rabot tovarishcha I. V. Stalina," Kniga i Proletarskaia Revoliutsiia, no. 12, 1939.

I--Izvestiia

LS--Leninskii Sbornik

Melikov--V. A. Melikov, Geroicheskaia oborona Tsaritsyna 1918 g. (Moscow: Voenizdat, 1938).

P--Pravda

Proletarskaia Revoliutsiia--Institut Marksa-Engelsa-Lenina, "Bibliografiia proizvedenii I. V. Stalina," Proletarskaia Revoliutsiia, no. 4, 1939.

S--I. V. Stalin, Sochineniia (Moscow: Gos. izd. pol. lit., 1946).

ZN--Zhizn' Natsional'nostei

PART ONE

1895 - 1934

PART I

INTRODUCTION

Stalin's significance as a historic figure has been growing in
recent years, thanks--inadvertently--to the efforts of Khrushchev.
While Stalin's successor shattered the incredible image of a deity-
vozhd', he thereby succeeded in enhancing the stature of Stalin the
historic dictator. To be told by Stalin's historians--as we once were--
that he was the genius of his age was not in itself justification for
regarding him as a major figure, but it is indeed worthy of serious
attention that later Soviet leaders and historians have regarded the
year of Stalin's death as a turning point only slightly less significant
than 1917 itself. This, too, may be a partisan and inadequate appraisal
of Soviet history, and the extent of the present essay does not permit
discussion of so broad a problem, but it is safe to say that as the
ludicrous and tragic Communist hagiography recedes, a new era in
non-Communist studies of Stalin begins.

The study of Stalin and the system with which he was so closely
associated remains, however, seriously hampered by the policies of
the Soviet Communist regimes during and after his lifetime. During the
period of Stalin hero-worship much was published concerning the leader,
but this revealed far more of the myth (probably a neglected subject in
its own right) than of the reality, which was distorted or suppressed in
a variety of ways. After the opening of the anti-Stalin campaign in
1956, some new and important information on the Stalinshchina was
disseminated, but the limits of such revelations, as thus far established,
still leave a great deal to be desired. While it lies within the power of
the present Moscow regime to reveal a great deal of previously

concealed material, it seems probable that the desire to avoid embarrassing stress on Stalin's role in Soviet history and the wish to conceal the responsibility of present leaders for his administration will inhibit frankness for years to come. Pending the beginning of a striking shift in Soviet treatment of their own political history, historians who are not subject to Communist party control are therefore faced with the need to cultivate such resources as are available at present, knowing that such efforts are bound to be far from complete--indeed, hoping that they will be rendered obsolete as soon as possible.

Clearly the papers of Stalin himself form one category of material on which studies relating to the leader must draw. Even if one could use all the Stalin papers that must exist in one place or another in the world, they would not form a self-sufficient basis for even a biographically oriented study, much less some broader theme. And in the present political circumstances the outsider's knowledge of this body of documentation must be considered even more limited in scholarly value. On the other hand, it is possible to amplify and to correct the picture of the Stalin papers provided by the thirteen volumes of the official Sochineniia, which was published in his lifetime and still serves as the most widely used guide on this subject.

Such is the objective of the present bibliography. In connection with doctoral work on an aspect of Stalin's ideas, I became aware that the official anthology was peppered with omissions and alterations and, quite obviously, was incomplete in relation to Stalin's life, for the published volumes in the series cover his papers only as far as January 1934. Not all of the problems that can be detected in this field can be solved, and it is probable that many others cannot even be detected, but I decided to see what could be done at present by way of amplification and correction.

This attempt is divided into two parts. The first part necessarily reflects the existence of the thirteen volumes of the official Sochineniia, covering Stalin's works through January 1934. The most interesting bibliographical work that is now feasible relates to this part of the whole, for the published materials attributable to Stalin in this period are fairly substantial, making it possible to question, amplify, and correct the Sochineniia to a considerable extent. The approach to the second part, the period from February 1934 to March 1953, is basically different in that there are no official Sochineniia volumes to consider and there is a much more limited body of Stalin papers to survey. This distinction in the source material is therefore marked by the division of the bibliography into two parts, and further discussion of the peculiarities of the second part occurs in a separate Introduction (see p. 149).

As for the first, larger, and more interesting part of this bibliography, it is well to begin by noting that there were several Soviet bibliographical efforts preceding the publication of Stalin's Sochineniia. These works cannot be used uncritically, but they are invaluable to the present survey and worth a few words of introductory comment. L. P. Beria's book (originally a series of lectures) K voprosu ob istorii bol'shevistskikh organizatsii v zakavkaz'e (Moscow, Gospolitizdat, 1935, and subsequent editions) is not primarily a bibliographical work, but it embodies a substantial amount of research bearing on the early, Georgian portion of any Stalin bibliography. As one would expect, this research was not executed personally by Beria. According to F. Makharadze--himself a historian of the party in Georgia and an object of Beria's criticisms--it was directed by the Georgian party boss at the Tiflis filial of the Marx-Engels-Lenin Institute, which reports to the Central Committee of the party.[1] One gathers that this investigation benefited by its sponsor's authority, which must have been sufficient to open all doors and drawers in Transcaucasia, and evidently it also

---

[1] F. Makharadze, "Pervye pechatnye trudy tovarishcha Stalina," Kniga i Proletarskaia Revoliutsiia, 1939, No. 12, p. 45.

benefited from expertise in the Georgian language beyond that readily
available in Russia proper. Understandably, Soviet bibliographers who
published at the close of the thirties leaned heavily on Beria's project
concerning Stalin's early publications in Georgian. One might have
supposed that when Volume I of the Sochineniia, containing most of the
works by Stalin in Georgian, appeared in 1946 it would have included
all the alleged Stalin papers cited by Beria. But such is not the case,
for twelve plausible Stalin documents (eleven originally written in
Georgian) that are specified in Beria's book do not appear in the
Sochineniia. Moreover, Beria did not back down in his attribution of
these documents to Stalin after the Sochineniia appeared, for the 1948
edition of Beria's book did not change any of these twelve attributions,
even though it was unable to cite their location in the Sochineniia, as it
was able to do, for the first time, in the case of some other documents.
With these two Stalinist scholarly works at loggerheads concerning the
authorship of twelve documents, there is little that the outsider can do
but call attention to the problem. Beria is hardly a trustworthy scholar,
and he had adequate careerist motivation to exaggerate Stalin's early
literary corpus. It does seem quite clear that Beria wrongly attributed
to Stalin several articles supposedly published in Russian (at a time
when Stalin was still publishing only in Georgian) in a newspaper called
Elizavetpol'skii Vestnik (whereas Stalin was never active in Elizavetpol)
On the other hand, the compilers of the Sochineniia can be proven to
have omitted a number of undoubted Stalin papers, including many listed
by earlier bibliographers, and it is true that Beria supports most of
his debatable attributions with alleged publication data, quotations, and
signatures (the last being especially convincing, if one can believe
Beria at all). Conceivably the entire discrepancy is explicable as part
of some subterranean conflict around 1946 among Stalin's lieutenants,
although this seems less than likely.

The next major development in bibliographical work concerning

Stalin consists of a cluster of publications more or less in honor of his sixtieth birthday in 1939. A modest sketch by L. Levin in that year mainly recalled the contents of the Stalin anthologies then in print and bemoaned the absence of more thorough bibliographical work.[2] But at this very time the situation was changing. Three research projects, one at the Lenin Library, one at the Marx-Engels-Lenin Institute, and one at the Institute of History of the Academy of Sciences, were consciously or otherwise competing for the honor of providing the first fairly thorough bibliography of the published papers of Stalin.[3]

These projects made an intensive effort to search all manner of Soviet publications for writings by Stalin through 1939. The resulting bibliographies prudently disclaimed completeness, and, indeed, they were not perfect with respect to Stalin documents appearing in Soviet publications. They did not dare consider the publications of Trotsky overseas and did not have access to any archival holdings, such as the Sochineniia later used. They also attributed to Stalin a few items that were almost certainly not his, though there might be some weak pretext for making the attribution. Still, these works set a new standard in the field of Stalin bibliography, and are in some ways more complete than the subsequent Sochineniia (granting, of course, that these bibliographers

---

[2]L. Levin, "Ob izdaniiakh i bibliograficheskikh ukazateliakh proizvedenii tovarishcha Stalina," Krasnyi Bibliotekar', 1939, No. 11-12, pp. 17-22.

[3]G. Z. Litvin-Molotova et al. (Gosudarstvennaia biblioteka imeni V.I. Lenina), "Bibliograficheskii ukazatel' rabot tovarishcha I.V. Stalina," Kniga i Proletarskaia Revoliutsiia, 1939, No. 12, pp. 126-158 (republished in Malaia Sovetskaia Entsiklopediia, 1940, X, 370-391); Institut Marksa-Engelsa-Lenina, "Bibliografiia proizvedenii I.V. Stalina," Proletarskaia Revoliutsiia, 1939, No. 4, pp. 171-209; A. Gurevich, "Perechen' vystuplenii i statei tovarishcha Stalina," Istoricheskii Zhurnal, 1940, No. 1, pp. 143-153. Of the three, the one in Proletarskaia Revoliutsiia is probably the best, being the only one to add data on the Georgian materials beyond Beria's research, and Gurevich's is the weakest, possibly a one-man enterprise.

did not reprint the body of the papers they listed). The present work, while not uncritical in its use of these bibliographies, could scarcely have been prepared without them.

These basic bibliographical surveys were subject to a critical review by a Soviet scholar named N. Anisimov, whose brief article is interesting for the gaps that it fills, or purports to fill.[4] Although Anisimov is annoying in his references to items that he attributes to Stalin without any specified substantiation, he did manage to find some plausible items that were overlooked by the others, and he seems to have had a superior grasp of the later findings of the Tiflis filial of the Marx-Engels-Lenin Institute. Less valuable is the larger and more pretentious book Stalin i o Staline, prepared by a group at the Leningrad Public Library under the direction of I. M. Iunover.[5] This includes a lengthy chronological list of Stalin's works through 1939 (pp. 129-200), but the greater part of the book consists of hagiographic filler, such as a special index of what Lenin said about Stalin and vice versa, and a list of Stalinist books about Stalin (there are other bibliographies of this latter sort, but they need not concern the present survey). Despite its length, this one Stalin bibliography in book format does not seem to add any new research; it depends wholly on earlier published bibliographical research and does not make full use of that.

In 1946 the first volume of Stalin's Sochineniia came off the press, presumably the immortal climax and conclusion of all bibliographical work on Stalin. In fact, it was much less--otherwise the present study would not be needed. Just how this series was prepared is not quite clear at present. Like one of the major bibliographies of

---

[4] N. Anisimov, "O bibliografii proizvedenii I. V. Stalina," Istorik Marksist, 1940, No. 1, pp. 115-117.

[5] Leningradskaia publichnaia biblioteka, Stalin i o Staline; ukazatel' literatury (Leningrad, Lenpartizdat, 1940).

1939, it was issued by the Marx-Engels-Lenin Institute, and it would seem probable that the editorial staff was partly the same; the 1939 bibliography might plausibly be supposed to be the first fruit of a single project leading to the Sochineniia. The contents, of the completed series and the earlier works are, however, sufficiently at variance to suggest the intervention of an additional editor-in-chief. In 1957 an official of the Marx-Engels-Lenin Institute told me that Stalin decided personally what was to be included in the collection, and it may be that a draft of the Sochineniia was drawn up on the basis of an amplified version of the birthday bibliographies, Stalin then deciding which items to include in the final product. Khrushchev told the Twentieth Party Congress that Stalin personally edited his own Kratkaia biografiia. If this is true, it should not be held incredible that he took time to make the final decisions on the contents of another major literary monument to his fame. It seems unlikely that any lesser personage would have dared to delete unquestionable Stalin papers from the collection, especially those that are seemingly orthodox.

The general introduction to the Sochineniia, signed by the Marx-Engels-Lenin Institute, does not give much indication of the problem of inclusiveness. It states that the collection will bring together "almost all" the works of Stalin, but it indicates neither the scope nor the basis of omissions (Sochineniia, I, vi), and even the claim to relative completeness would be hard to justify. To be sure, almost all of the major doctrinal writings of Stalin are included in the Sochineniia; all of the items appearing in Voprosy leninizma and similar standard anthologies are included. Some of the omissions, however, are not without considerable doctrinal interest, and in terms of gross verbiage a fairly sizable portion of Stalin's writings is missing. If one measures the omissions in terms of separate items, noting all the very minor bits, the selectivity of the Sochineniia is still more striking. In the present list of Stalin papers to February 1934 there are, in all, 895 separate entries, of which only about 480 appeared in the first thirteen volumes of the Sochineniia. Such an aggregative statement should not be taken too seriously, for there may be valid reasons for not attributing to Stalin some items in the list, and one might sympathize with the compilers of the official volumes in their exclusion of the trivia. (One might sympathize more, were it not for the inclusion of a quantity of trivia in the official volumes and the absence of any explanation of the basis of th selectivity.) In any case, the careful scholar should be aware of the existence of the problem, and he may wish to consider the general incidence of omissions from the Sochineniia.

For the period in Stalin's career up to 1910, during which Transcaucasia was his main base of operations, numbers of writings are omitted from the Sochineniia, as was mentioned earlier in connection with the Beria book. References in Beria and a variety of other Soviet publications indicate that Stalin wrote about 110 different articles, leaflets, letters, or other papers during his Transcaucasian years. Of these, 56 are included in the Sochineniia; the rest are not. I have not had access to the kind of materials necessary to determine with any certainty whether the Sochineniia is really as deficient in this as Beria and other Soviet sources indicate, or, for that matter, whether the attributions to Stalin in the Sochineniia are reliable or not. Probably the best general advice is to regard with skepticism most items attributed to Stalin on the basis of a committee signature or no signature during this period, while accepting with some confidence items signed by one of the pseudonyms, such as "Koba" or "Besoshvili," which Stalin was almost certainly using in this period. On this basis one might conclude that some of the early attributions to Stalin that appear in the Sochineniia are unreliable, while a goodly number of items that really were by Stalin are omitted.

The pre-Revolutionary years of Stalin's career after he left Transcaucasia are much more fully represented in the Sochineniia. In

one case it is clear that an article by Stalin on Duma tactics was suppressed in the Sochineniia because he was too soft on a Polish socialist
(see item 134). In another there is an undoubted omission of a short
but staunchly Leninist article for no apparent reason (see item 136).
There are a few other definite omissions, but not nearly as many as
in the Transcaucasian years or the period of revolution and civil war.

For the months between the February and October Revolutions
the present listing includes 96 items, of which 77 appear in the
Sochineniia. Those that are published in the official anthology include
almost all the articles by Stalin in the press. The more interesting
omissions are records of what Stalin said in various meetings, such
as the party conference of March 29, 1917 (see item 152) and the
Bolshevik military conference of June 17 (see item 170). Once Stalin
was in power, however, the range of his new responsibilities involved
him in a host of administrative and military activities which were reflected in a greatly increased volume of paperwork bearing his signature, and of this the Sochineniia includes rather little, compared to
that which eventually was published in one place or another. Considering the problems of co-signatories, purely formal signatures, and
mere trivia, one may readily sympathize with the compilers of the
Sochineniia up to a point. The problem is that at times co-signatures,
formality, or triviality did not deter the compilers from including
material, while at many other times some broad policy of selectivity
does seem to have been at work. No quantitative statement about this
can be adequate, owing to the number of borderline cases, but it is
roughly accurate to say that between the October Revolution and the
end of 1922 there are about 120 known letters, telegrams, orders, and
the like attributable to Stalin, of which only about 30 appear in the
Sochineniia. Particularly interesting is the high rate of omission of
communications from Stalin to Lenin, notwithstanding the inclusion of
some very brief items of this type (e.g., see item 474). Only sixteen

of about fifty published communications from Stalin to Lenin during the period 1918-1922 are included, even though there is no apparent cause for embarrassment in the content of most of the exclusions. Considering the immense effort that was once made to show Stalin's close association with Lenin, this is puzzling, unless it is possible to argue that Stalin found the kind of association revealed in these communications, taken as a whole, too obviously that of a captain with one of his lieutenants.

In these first post-revolutionary years there is an interesting cluster of omissions from the Sochineniia which deal with the question of nationality, Stalin's speciality in internal administration. About a dozen papers bearing on this topic are omitted. These do not concern much that is of basic doctrinal importance, but there are some interesting documents on practical administrative problems among them. In some cases it is fairly clear why Stalin wished to disassociate himself from them. On two notable occasions tactical considerations impelled him to take a fairly conciliatory attitude toward Ukrainian "bourgeois" nationalists (see items 243, 536), which in the long run probably appeared rather unseemly for one who wished to be considered an unwavering Leninist. On the other hand, there are some omitted documents that might make the alleged builder of the fraternal union of Soviet nationalities appear rather harsh in his approach to minority nationalities. This is especially true of Stalin's reply to Lenin's critique of the proposal that the U.S.S.R. be formed by bringing the Ukrainian, Belorussian, and Transcaucasian Soviet Republics into the existing Russian Soviet Federative Socialist Republic--a proposal favored by Stalin (see item 612). In the reply Stalin displayed not only a rather disrespectful attitude toward Lenin, but also a contempt for the kind of federation that eventually was adopted and which he cynically praised. It may be added that we can be quite certain that the document in question was known to Soviet researchers from their own archives

and not only as a publication of Trotsky, in whose archives it is pre-
served. In 1956 the availability of the document in Moscow was attested
by references to it in an article in Voprosy Istorii (see item 612).

The years 1923-1933 are less replete with omissions in the
Sochineniia. Although it is safe to guess that Stalin continued to produce a wide variety of papers, it seems that those not intended for
early publication generally went into files that were under Stalin's
direct control, in contrast to the situation prevailing in the first years
of Soviet power. (For instance, many of the Stalin documents of 1918-
1922 went into Lenin's files and were available to the editors of the
serial Leninskii Sbornik, which published them.) Yet, some of the significant articles or speeches by Stalin that were published in the Soviet
press in 1923-1933 were omitted from the Sochineniia, evidently for
reasons of politics rather than technical editorial considerations.
Several interesting items bearing on Comintern politics are notable
among the omissions, including the longest single known work by Stalin
to be suppressed in the Sochineniia: a series of speeches in May 1929
on the American Communist party (see item 820). Having no special
knowledge of Soviet-American Communist relations, I cannot explain
this suppression; nor does Theodore Draper explain it in American
Communism in Soviet Russia (New York, Viking Press, 1960, pp. 409-
412).

By the early thirties Stalin was sufficiently deified to be the
recipient of many published letters from obscure Soviet citizens, usually
reporting various achievements, and he answered a number of these.
How he determined which letters he would answer is hard to say. What
further caprice or logic led to the inclusion of some of these answers,
but not all, in the Sochineniia is still more puzzling; this does not,
however, seem to be a matter of great importance.

In general, it may be reliably stated that Stalin's Sochineniia
omitted a considerable quantity of rather varied material that deserves

to be in a complete collection. The present survey lists such omissions as can be identified precisely (granting that the authenticity of all items is not determinate), but can do nothing about the unpublished documents which can be assumed to exist, but cannot be described or enumerated. That such a body of papers exists can be definitively established by scattered archival references in Soviet historical literature, occasional in Stalin's later years (e.g., in E. B. Genkin, Obrazovanie SSR [Moscow, 1947], p. 79) and somewhat more frequently since he died (e.g., in S. F. Naida, O nekotorykh voprosakh istorii grazhdanskoi voiny v SSSR [Moscow, 1958], p. 226, which tantalizingly refers to the "Centra Party Archives, Stalin Collection"). Khrushchev revealed a few bits of Stalin's official correspondence in the course of his "secret" speech to the Twentieth Party Congress, and it seems likely that a substantial volume of his papers, mostly from his years of supreme power, were kept on file, for most foreign visitors gained the impression that the dictator kept a well organized secretariat.

The compilers of the Sochineniia seem to have had access to at least some material of this sort (unlike the earlier Soviet bibliographer for the collection includes a substantial number of papers of various sorts that were previously unpublished. Since one cannot confirm the authenticity of these items by examining the original documents, the possibility that they may have been fabricated is worth considering. On the whole, available evidence does not suggest that this is likely. All documents alleged by the Sochineniia to have been previously published do, in fact, turn up in the expected places, so far as can be determined with available library resources. Introductory comments in the official volumes sometimes refer to documents that were sought but not discovered (e.g., an essay on the nationality question composed in 1915), which is some assurance that the compilers (or Stalin) did not fabricate what they could not find. And neither Trotsky nor Khrushchev has accused Stalin of inventing retroactively his own words (suppressing or altering them is, of course, another matter). One may wonder how he came to take time from pressing business in March 1929 to compose a lengthy essay on the problem of nationality, addressed to some obscure comrades, and then not bother to publish it for almost twenty years (see item 819). But caprice seems to crop up in various ways in the course of this investigation, and there seems to be no special motivation for the possible predating of this work.

Another question related to such publications from the archives is the anonymity of the addressee of several letters written by Stalin after the Revolution, when the need for security against Tsarist police had passed (e.g., see item 755). If the letters were fabricated at a later date, a meaningless name could equally well have been fabricated. Or were the real addressees the victims of later purges, making them persons to whom Stalin could not have been writing a letter, according to the rules of double-think? In the case of a letter "to Comrade M--ert" (see item 675) it is believed that the original addressee, A. Maslow, was displaced because he became a "deviator" and that letters hinting the addressee to have been another (German) Communist, Mehnert, were inserted.

Although on the whole it is impossible to determine the extent to which the Sochineniia distorts documents published from the archives, it is possible to compare the texts of many documents as they appear in the official anthology and in their earliest available published form. To make a perfectly reliable analysis of this problem would require a greater appetite for word-by-word comparison of texts than I could muster, but a fairly arduous attempt in this direction did reveal numerous and widely scattered alterations, of which only the more important are noted in the bibliographical listing. The changes fall into four principal categories. First, there are rather numerous improvements in style (not noted in the bibliographical listing). Stalin's Russian in the years before he approached the heights of power often suffered from poor usage or construction; later he improved, or his staff

15

improved his work before it went to press. A certain amount of polish
ing was applied to many compositions of early date before they were
recorded for posterity--which is not to say that Stalin's finished litera
products were ever graceful.

A second category of changes, rarely encountered, consists of
corrections of factual statements, such as occasional statistical
references; these are not particularly significant.

A third category, which might be labeled "matters of Bolshevik
etiquette, " includes the systematic removal of the title of "tovarishch"
before the names of persons who fell victim to the purges and some
verbal changes that cannot be considered simply matters of literary
style. As an example of the latter, the somewhat Great Russian im-
perialist use of "tuzemtsy" with reference to various nationalities was
replaced with the more tolerant term "mestnye korennye zhiteli" or
something similar.

Finally, there is the fourth category, covering all changes of
genuinely substantive character. It is chiefly this type of change that is
noted in the bibliographical listing, and since these changes are quite
diverse in their specifics, it is hardly possible to characterize them,
except to note that the political motivation is generally fairly obvious.

In sum, Stalin's Sochineniia falls far short of the standards
that one would hope for in a definitive collection of a statesman's
papers. The present attempt to ameliorate this situation has drawn
upon the Soviet publications previously noted, upon other Soviet publications that might contain additional Stalin papers (including quite a
thorough scanning of Pravda and Bol'shevik during the period of Stalin's
life), upon non-Soviet secondary literature which contains references
to Stalin, upon the Trotsky Archives at the Houghton Library of the
Harvard College Library (the only bits of previously unpublished
material used), and upon the advice of various scholars. The result
must have shortcomings that reflect not only the investigator's

exclusion from Soviet archives, but also his inability to find all possible open sources. If publication of this bibliography inspires
specialists to call attention to various addenda, it will be all to the
good.

Concerning the inclusiveness of this bibliography, several
points are in order, for it is no simple matter to determine what
should be considered fit for inclusion in even an undiscriminating
listing of Stalin's presumed works. On the whole, Part I of the present
work takes a broad view of what might be attributed to Stalin, including even trivia (one document is merely a receipt for official funds)
and certain items that are probably not Stalin's work in any personal
sense (such as papers bearing multiple signatures). This approach is
justified partly by the fact that the bibliography is meant to amplify
the Sochineniia, which itself includes some trivia and some items with
multiple signatures, and partly by the desire to leave a final judgment
to individual users, who may possess additional information. A special
problem is posed by a number of official documents, such as decrees
and military orders, which Stalin signed, but which may not represent
his work in any specific sense. In Part II many items of this sort are
omitted from the main listing since it is quite clear that the signature
of the Leader was in many cases simply used as a kind of official seal.
But in the early days of Stalin's career as an administrator and military-
political leader his position was not so lofty and it is known that he had
a very small staff most of that time.[6] In these circumstances it is
likely that he stood much closer to paperwork bearing his signature

---

[6] For example, see the following descriptions of the scanty or-
ganization that was the People's Commissariat for Nationality Affairs
in its early days: S. Pestkovskii, "Kak sozdavalsia Narkomnats,"
Zhizn' Natsional'nostei, 1923, I, 272-273 and Peskovstikii, "Vospominaniia o rabote v Narkomnatse," Proletarskaia Revoliutsiia, 1930,
No. 6, pp. 124-131.

and personally took part in the drafting of a number of decrees and similar documents. It therefore seems best to include items of this sort, granting that it is unlikely that all represent Stalin's personal work.

The latitudinarianism of this bibliography is, however, not unlimited. Some attributions to Stalin that occur in the Soviet bibliographies are not included here. For example, a reference in the bibliography of 1939 appearing in Proletarskaia Revoliutsiia to two proclamations of 1902 leads one to the book Batumskaia demonstratsiia 1902 g. (Moscow, Partizdat, 1937), where one finds only the documents without the slightest suggestion that they were Stalin's work in any way, although the book as a whole is certainly devoted to the magnification of Stalin's role in the demonstration. Quite a different question concerns a number of documents attributed to Stalin by various Soviet listings on the basis of initials serving as signatures to published articles. For example, Anisimov attributes to Stalin an article entitled "Kazusnoe 'Delo,'" which appeared in Pravda July 6, 1912, over the signature of "K.S." It is true that as recently as April 1912 Stalin had used this signature, derived from his pseudonyms "Koba" and "Stalin." It seems, however, that he changed over to other signatures by the end of April and never again returned to "K.S.," probably to avoid identification with another Bolshevik writer, who repeatedly used those initials from 1912 until at least 1918. Moreover, Stalin was arrested in late April of 1912 and did not escape until September; meanwhile, he wrote nothing (if one excludes the alleged "K.S." article), as was his custom when in custody. It seems quite clear that a number of articles, which might be attributed to Stalin if one assumed that he was "K.S." in every usage of those initials, should not in fact be considered his.

In concluding this Introduction, it may be said that the preparation of such a bibliography is really a shot in the dark. The compiler cannot know in advance by whom or how it may be found useful. If it were clear that this collection of information would serve one or a few specific studies, it would be better simply to prepare such studies and not to bother with the tedious and cumbersome work of editing a bibliography like this one. But in fact the present data is in a sense too narrow to be used as the main basis for some new monograph, and at the same time is so diverse that it might conceivably be useful to a wide variety of scholars, if only to save them some effort./

1.   Poems. (Trans. from the Georgian.)
          In Iberia, 1895-1896, according to Kelendzheridze, E.
     "Stikhi iunogo Stalina" in Rasskazy o velikom Staline* (Tiflis:
     Zaria Vostoka, 1941), pp. 67-70. See also Robert Payne, The
     Rise and Fall of Stalin. New York, Simon and Shuster, 1965,
     pp. 47-51.

                              1900

2.   Tovarishchi. [Comrades.] (Trans. from the Georgian.)
          Leaflet published by the Tiflis Social Democratic Group
     concerning the strike of the Transcaucasian railroad workers
     in August 1900, according to Anisimov, p. 116 (no explanation
     or authentication offered).

                              1901

3.   Ot redaktsii. [From the Editors.] (Trans. from the Georgian.)
          Unsigned article in Brdzola, no. 1, Sept., 1901.
     I, 3-10.

4.   Rossiiskaia Sotsial-Demokraticheskaia Partiia i ee blizhaishie
     zadachi. [The Russian Social-Democratic Party and Its Immedi-
     ate Tasks.] (Trans. from the Georgian.)
          Unsigned article in Brdzola, nos. 2-3, Nov.-Dec., 1901.
     I, 11-31.

                              1902

5.   Tovarishchi rabochie! [Comrade Workers!] (Trans. from the
     Georgian.)
          Proclamation, signed "Batumskaia Sotsialdemokraticheskai

----

*Prior to February, 1918, all dates are Old Style.

Gruppa, " dated June 10, 1902, republished in Batumskaia demonstratsiia 1902 goda (Moscow: Partizdat, 1937) pp. 27-30, attributing it to Stalin without any substantiation.

6. Tovarishchi rabochie! [Comrade Workers!] (Trans. from the Georgian.)

Proclamation, signed "Batumskaia Sotsial-Demokratiche kaia Gruppa," dated June 29, 1902, republished in Batums-kaia demonstratsiia 1902 goda, (Moscow: Partizdat, 1937), pp. 30-33, attributing it to Stalin without any substantiation.

1904

7. Kak ponimaet Sotsial-Demokratiia natsional'nyi vopros? [The Social-Democratic View of the National Question.] (Trans. from the Georgian.)

Unsigned article in Proletariatis Brdzola, no. 7, Sept. 1, 1904.
I, 32-55.

8. Letter to M. Davitashvili. (Trans. from the Georgian.)

S. says this letter found in Russian trans. in Lenin-Krupskaia archives, addressed to Georgian Social Democrat living in Leipzig. First published in S. No information on signature. Written Sept.-Oct., 1904.
I, 56-58.

9. Letter to M. Davitashvili. (Trans. from the Georgian.)

Written Oct., 1904. Otherwise remarks on preceding entry apply.
I, 59-61.

10. Tretii s"ezd pered sudom kavkazskikh "Men'shevikov." [The Third Congress before the Court of the Caucasian "Mensheviks. (Trans. from the Georgian.)

Proletariatis Brdzola, no. 9, 1905. Republished in Proletarii, no. 14, Aug. 16, 1905, without signature or other attribution to any individual. Anisimov, p. 117, attributes this to Stalin without further explanation. Internal evidence inconclusive, although it sounds somewhat as if author had been at Third Congress (Stalin was not) and had a fuller general picture of party affairs than Stalin usually displays at this time. The article is staunchly Leninist and cannot have been suppressed because of any "deviation."

11.   Proclamation on Armenian-Tatar conflict.
        Attributed to Stalin by Anisimov, p. 116. He asserts it was printed Nov. 1904, by Caucasian Union Committee, but gives no information on basis of attribution to Stalin.

1905

12.   Klass proletariev i partiia proletariev. [The Proletarian Class and the Proletarian Party.] (Trans. from the Georgian.)
        Unsigned article in Proletariatis Brdzola, no. 8, Jan. 1, 1905.
I, 62-73.

13.   Rabochie Kavkaza, pora otomstit'! [Workers of the Caucasus, It Is Time to Take Revenge!] (Trans. from the Georgian.)
        Manifesto of Jan. 8, 1905, signed "Soiuznyi komitet."
I, 74-80.

14.   Vremennoe revoliutsionnoe pravitel'stvo i nasha taktika. [The Provisional Revolutionary Government and Our Tactics.] (Trans. from the Georgian.)
        Proletariatis Brdzola, no. 9, 1905, according to Anisimov, p. 116, who does not explain why Stalin may be considered the author, except to note that the point of view of this article conforms to Lenin's "Dve taktiki Sotsial-Demokratii v demokraticheskoi revoliutsii."

15.   Da zdravstvuet mezhdunarodnoe bratstvo! [Long Live International Fraternity!] (Trans. from the Georgian.)
        Proclamation dated Feb. 13, 1905, signed "Tiflisskii komitet."
I, 81-3.

16.   K grazhdanam. Da zdravstvuet krasnoe znamia! [To Citizens.
Long Live the Red Flag!] (Trans. from the Georgian.)
    Proclamation dated Feb. 15, 1905, signed "Tiflisskii
    komitet."
I, 84-8.

17.   Chto vyiasnilos'? [What Was Made Clear?.] (Presumably
trans. from the Georgian.)
    Proclamation of "Kavkazskii soiuznyi komitet" dated
    Mar. 26, 1905, according to Beria, 90-94, which appears
    to reproduce the entire document.

18.   Korotko o partiinykh raznoglasiiakh. [Briefly about the Disagre
ments in the Party.] (Trans. from the Georgian.)
    Pamphlet of the Caucasian Union Committee published
    May, 1905.
I, 89-130.

19.   Vooruzhennoe vosstanie i nasha taktika. [Armed Insurrection
and Our Tactics.] (Trans. from the Georgian.)
    Unsigned article in Proletariatis Brdzola, no. 10, July 1
    1905.
I, 131-7.

20.   Nachali za zdravie, konchili za upokoi. [They Began Well and
Finished Badly.] (Trans. from the Georgian.)
    Proletariatis Brdzola, no. 11, Aug. 15, 1905. Attributed
    to Stalin by Beria, who gives excerpts pp. 72-73. No evi-
    dence of signature.

21.   Tsarskii manifest i narodnaia revoliutsiia. [The Tsar's Mani-
festo and the People's Revolution.] (Trans. from the Georgian.
    Proletariatis Brdzola, no. 11, Aug. 15, 1905. Attributed
    to Stalin by Anisimov on basis of article in Proletaruli revo-
    lutsia, no. 1, 1939, published by Tiflis filial (branch) of
    Marx-Engels-Lenin Institute. No evidence on signature.

22.   Vremennoe revoliutsionnoe pravitel'stvo i Sotsial-Demokratiia.
[The Provisional Revolutionary Government and Social Democ-
racy.] (Trans. from the Georgian.)
    Unsigned article in Proletariatis Brdzola, no. 11, Aug. 1
    1905, continuing with unfinished sequel not published until S.
I, 138-159.

23.   Otvet "Sotsial-Demokratu." [A Reply to the Social-Democrat.]
       (Trans. from the Georgian.)
              Unsigned article in Proletariatis Brdzola, no. 11,
          Aug. 15, 1905.
       I, 160-172.

24.   Reaktsiia usilivaetsia. [Reaction Is Growing.] (Trans. from
       the Georgian.)
              Unsigned article in Proletariatis Brdzola, no. 12, Oct. 15,
          1905.
       I, 173-178.

25.   Burzhuaziia stavit lovushku. [The Bourgeoisie Is Laying a Trap.]
       (Trans. from the Georgian.)
              Unsigned article in Proletariatis Brdzola, no. 12, Oct. 15,
          1905.
       I, 179-184.

26.   Grazhdane! [Citizens!]
              Proclamation signed "Tiflisskii komitet," published in
          Oct. 1905.

27.   Speech to workers' meeting at Nadzaladevi, Tiflis, on the day
       of the proclamation of the October Manifesto. (Presumably
       trans. from the Georgian.)
              Beria, p. 104, gives excerpts on basis of material in ar-
          chives of Tiflis filial of Marx-Engels-Lenin Institute.

28.   Ko vsem rabochim. [To All the Workers.] (Trans. from the
       Georgian.)
              Proclamation signed Oct. 19, 1905, "Tiflisskii komitet."
       I, 189-192.

29.   Tiflis, 20-go noiabria, 1905 g. [Tiflis, November 20, 1905.]
              Unsigned article in Kavkazskii Rabochii Listok, Nov. 20,
          1905.
       I, 193-195.

30.   K soldatam. [To the Soldiers.] (Presumably trans. from the
       Georgian.)

Proclamation, Nov., 1905, signed "Tiflisskii komitet, " according to Beria, p. 93. However, the 1948 edition of this book does not include this attribution, unlike all others cited in this bibliography on the basis of Beria. (Note that 4th ed., 1938, is used for attributions in this bibliography.)

31. Resolution at Tammerfors Party Conference, Dec. 12-17, 1905.
Signed by Lenin, Zimin, Voronov, Ivanovich [Stalin] and Emel'ianov. Stalin's signature presumably implies merely adherence and not co-authorship. Published in VKP (b) v rezoliutsiiakh i resheniiakh s''ezdov, konferentsii i plenumov tsentral'nogo komiteta*(Moscow: Gos. izd. pol. lit., 1940), I, p. 59.

1906

32. Izveshcheniia ob Obshcherossiiskikh Konferentsiiakh Bol'shinstva i Men'shinstva. [Notice on the All-Russian Conference of the Majority and the Minority.] (Presumably trans. from the Georgian.)
Pamphlet of Jan., 1906, signed "Kavkazskii soiuznyi komitet, " according to Anisimov, p. 116 (no explanation or evidence offered).

33. Dve skhvatki. [Two Clashes.] (Trans. from the Georgian.)
Pamphlet of Jan. 7, 1906, evidently unsigned.
I, 196-205.

34. Ne tsarskaia reforma, a narodnaia revoliutsiia. [Not a Tsarist Reform, but a People's Revolution.] (Presumably trans. from the Georgian.)
Proclamation of Feb., 1906, signed "Tiflisskii ob''edinennyi komitet RSDRP, " according to Beria, pp. 119-122, where it is evidently reproduced in full.

35. Gosudarstvennaia Duma i taktika Sotsial-Demokratii. [The State Duma and the Tactics of the Social-Democratic Party.] (Trans. from the Georgian.)
Article in Gantiadi, no. 3, Mar. 8, 1906, signed J. Besoshvili.
I, 206-213.

36. Partiia 'Nezavisimtsev' i zadacha Sotsial-Demokratii. [The Part of 'Independents' and the Tasks of the Social-Democratic Party.] (Trans. from the Georgian.)

  Article signed "I. Besoshvili" in Gantiadi, no. 5, Mar. 10, 1906, according to Beria, pp. 78, 81.

37. Politicheskie khameleony. [Political Chameleons.] (Trans. from the Georgian.)

  Article signed "Besoshvili" in Elva, no. 3, Mar. 15, 1906, according to Beria, pp. 82-83, which includes a substantial excerpt.

38. Agrarnyi vopros. [The Agrarian Question.] (Trans. from the Georgian.)

  Article signed "I. Besoshvili" in Elva, nos. 5, 9, 10, Mar. 17, 22, 23, 1906.

  I, 214-229.

39. Eshche o khameleonakh. [More about Chameleons.] (Trans. from the Georgian.)

  Article signed "Besoshvili" in Elva, no. 5, Mar. 17, 1906, according to Proletarskaia Revoliutsiia, p. 173.

40. Eshche raz o khameleonakh. [Once More about Chameleons.] (Trans. from the Georgian.)

  Article signed "Besoshvili" in Elva, no. 7, Mar. 19, 1906, according to Proletarskaia Revoliutsiia, p. 173.

41. K agrarnomu voprosu. [Concerning the Agrarian Question.] (Trans. from the Georgian.)

  Article signed "I. Besoshvili" in Elva, no. 14, Mar. 29, 1906.

42. Statements at Fourth Party Congress, Apr. 10-25, 1906.

  O peresmotre agrarnoi programmy. [The Revision of the Agrarian Program.] Speech in seventh session, Apr. 13, 1906, published in Chetvertyi (ob''edinitel'nyi) s''ezd RSDRP. Protokoly* (Moscow: Partizdat, 1934).

  I, 236-238.

Statement in discussion during ninth session, published in Protokoly, p. 149 (the editors of Protokoly state that it is impossible to assign a precise date to each session).

O tekushchem momente. [The Present Situation.] Speech in fifteenth session, April 17, 1906, published in Protokoly I, 239-240.

Statement in discussion during eighteenth session, published in Protokoly, pp. 326-327.

Written statement submitted during the nineteenth session, published in Protokoly, p. 347.

Another written statement submitted during the nine-teenth session, published in Protokoly, p. 349.

Written statement submitted during twenty-fifth session, published in Protokoly, p. 463.

43. Chto delat'? [What Is to Be Done?] (Trans. from the Georgian.
        Article signed "Koba" in Akhali Tskhovreba, no. 1,
        June 20, 1906, according to Proletarskaia Revoliutsiia,
        p. 173.

44. Anarkhizm ili sotsializm? [Anarchism or Socialism?] (Trans.
     from the Georgian.)
        I, 373-392 (here listed as "Prilozhenie" [appendix] to
        longer version of article, bearing same title, which appears
        at a later date; the longer version is listed as No. 61 in the
        present bibliography).

        Serialized article signed "Koba" in Akhali Tskhovreba,
        nos. 2, 4, 7 and 16 dated June 21, 24, 28, and July 9, 1906.

45. Reorganizatsiia v Tiflise. [Reorganization in Tiflis.] (Trans.
     from the Georgian.)
        Article signed "Koba" in Akhali Tskhovreba, no. 5,
        June 25, 1906, according to Beria, pp. 79-80, which in-
        cludes excerpts.

46.   Sotsialisticheskii proletariat i revoliutsionnoe krest'ianstvo.
      [The Socialist Proletariat and the Revolutionary Peasantry.]
      (Trans. from the Georgian.)
            Article signed "Koba" in Akhali Tskhovreba, no. 6,
      June 27, 1906, according to Proletarskaia Revoliutsiia,
      p. 173.

47.   Ulitsa zagovorila! [The Street Began to Speak!] (Trans. from
      the Georgian.)
            Article signed "Koba" in Akhali Tskhovreba, no. 8,
      June 29, 1906, according to Proletarskaia Revoliutsiia,
      p. 173.

48.   V chem oshibki t. Brodiagi? [In What Is Comrade Brodiaga
      Mistaken?] (Trans. from the Georgian.)
            Article in Akhali Tskhovreba, July 2, 1906, according
      to F. Makharadze, "Pervye pechatnye trudy tovarishcha
      Stalina," Kniga i Proletarskaia Revoliutsiia, 1939, no. 12,
      p. 40.

49.   Gegemoniia proletariata i nyneshnei revoliutsii. [The Hegemony
      of the Proletariat and the Present Revolution.] (Trans. from
      the Georgian.)
            Article signed "Koba" in Akhali Tskhovreba, no. 11,
      July 4, 1906, according to Proletarskaia Revoliutsiia, p.
      173.

50.   Professional'nye Soiuzy v Tiflise. [The Trade Unions in Tiflis.]
      (Trans. from the Georgian.)
            Article in Akhali Tskhovreba, no. 12, July 5, 1906,
      according to Beria, pp. 80-81, which includes excerpts but
      no information on signature.

51.   Nashi raznoglasiia. 1. Ulitsa i Duma. 2. Revoliutsiia i Reforma.
      [Our Disagreements. 1. The Street and the Duma. 2. The
      Revolution and the Reform.] (Trans. from the Georgian.)
            Serialized article signed "Koba" in Akhali Tskhovreba,
      nos. 14 and 16, July 7 and 9, 1906, according to
      Proletarskaia Revoliutsiia, p. 173.

52. Reaktsiia ozhestochaetsia, tesnee ob''ediniaites'! [The Re-
action Is Hardening, Unite More Firmly!] (Trans. from the
Georgian.)
  Article in <u>Akhali Tskhovreba</u>, no. 17, July 11, 1906,
according to Beria, p. 129, which includes excerpt but no
information on signature.

53. Razognannaia Duma i Ob''edinennaia Ulitsa. [The Dispersed
Duma and the United Street.] (Trans. from the Georgian.)
  Article in <u>Akhali Tskhovreba</u>, no. 18, July 12, 1906,
according to Beria, p. 129, which includes excerpts but no
information on signature.

54. Marks i Engel's o vosstanii. [Marx and Engels on Insurrection.]
(Trans. from the Georgian.)
  Article signed "Koba" in <u>Akhali Tskhovreba</u>, no. 19,
July 13, 1906.
I, 241-246.

55. Mezhdunarodnaia kontrrevoliutsiia. [International Counter-
revolution.] (Trans. from the Georgian.)
  Article signed "Koba" in <u>Akhali Tskhovreba</u>, no. 20,
July 14, 1906.
I, 247-249.

56. Sovremennyi moment i Ob''edinitel'nyi S''ezd Rabochei Partii.
[The Present Situation and the Unity Congress of the Workers'
Party.] (Trans. from the Georgian.)
  Pamphlet signed "Comrade K.," published in July or
August, 1906.
I, 250-276.

57. Klassovaia bor'ba. [The Class Struggle.] (Trans. from the
Georgian.)
  Article signed "Ko..." in <u>Akhali Droeba</u>, no. 1, Nov. 14,
1906.
I, 277-285.

58. Mestnyi tsentr rabochikh professional'nykh soiuzov. [The Local
Center of the Workers' Trade Unions.] (Trans. from the
Georgian.)
  Article signed "Ko..." in <u>Akhali Droeba</u>, no. 2, Nov. 20,
1906, according to <u>Proletarskaia Revoliutsiia</u>, p. 174.

59. Neskol'ko slov o Tiflisskom Professional'nom Soiuze Prikazchika.
     [A Few Words about the Tiflis Trade Union of Shop Stewards.]
     (Trans. from the Georgian.)
          Article in Akhali Droeba, no. 3, Nov. 27, 1906, accord-
     ing to G. Sturua, "Professional'noe dvizhenie v Gruzii,"
     Voprosy profdvizheniia, no. 3, 1937, 43.

60. "Fabrichnoe zakonodatel'stvo" i proletarskaia bor'ba. ["Factory
     Legislation" and the Proletarian Struggle.] (Trans. from the
     Georgian.)
          Article signed "Ko..." in Akhali Droeba, no. 4, Dec. 4, 1906.
     I, 286-293.

61. Anarkhizm ili sotsializm? [Anarchism or Socialism?] (Trans.
     from the Georgian.)
          Serialized article signed "Ko..." in Akhali Droeba, nos.
     5, 6, 7, 8, Dec. 11, 18, 25, 1906; Chveni Tskhovreba, nos.
     3, 5, 8, 9, Jan. 1, Feb. 21, 23, 27, 28, 1907; Dro, nos. 21
     22, 23, 26, April 4, 5, 6, 10, 1907. There is a longer ver-
     sion of the article listed under No. 44.
     I, 294-372.

1907

62. Preface to the Georgian edition of Kautsky's pamphlet, "The
     Driving Forces and the Prospects of the Russian Revolution."
          Preface dated Feb. 10, 1907, signed "Koba."
     II, 1-13.

63. Nyneshnee polozhenie. [The Present Situation.] (Trans. from
     the Georgian.)
          Article in Chveni Takhovreba, no. 1, according to
     Anisimov, p. 115, on basis of article in publication of Tiflis
     filial (branch) of Marx-Engels-Lenin Institute, Proletaruli
     Revolutsia, no. 1, 1939. No information on signature.

64. Izbiratel'naia bor'ba v Peterburge i Men'sheviki. [The Election
     Campaign in St. Petersburg and the Mensheviks.] (Trans. from
     the Georgian.)
          Unsigned article in Chveni Tskhovreba, no. 1, Feb. 18,
     1907.
     II, 14-19.

65. Stolypinskaia deklaratsiia. [The Stolypin Declaration.] (Trans. from the Georgian.)

> Unsigned article in Dro, no. 1, March 11, 1907, according to Proletarskaia Revoliutsiia, p. 174.

66. Preniia po povodu goloda. [The Debate on the Cause of the Famine.] (Trans. from the Georgian.)

> Unsigned article in Dro, no. 1, Mar. 11, 1907, according to Proletarskaia Revoliutsiia, p. 174.

67. Sovety vraga dlia nas gibel'ny. [The Enemy's Advice Is Ruinous for Us.]

> Unsigned article in Dro, no. 2, March 13, 1907, according to Proletarskaia Revoliutsiia, p. 174.

68. Samoderzhavie kadetov ili samoderzhavie naroda? [The Autocracy of the Kadets or the Sovereignty of the People?] (Trans. from the Georgian.)

> Unsigned article in Dro, no. 2, Mar. 13, 1907. II, 20-21.

69. Piatyi s''ezd Sotsial-Demokraticheskoi Partii. [The Fifth Congress of the Social-Democratic Party.] (Trans. from the Georgian.)

> Unsigned article in Dro, nos. 2 and 4, Mar. 13 and 15, 1907, according to Proletarskaia Revoliutsiia, p. 174.

70. Chto ne nravitsia vragu v nas--to polezno dlia nas. [What the Enemy Dislikes in Us Is Beneficial for Us.] (Trans. from the Georgian.)

> Unsigned article in Dro, no. 4, Mar. 15, 1907, according to Proletarskaia Revoliutsiia, p. 174.

71. Korrektorskaia oshibka ili blankizm? [A Proof-Reader's Error or Blanquiism?] (Trans. from the Georgian.)

> Unsigned article in Dro, no. 4, Mar. 15, 1907, according to Proletarskaia Revoliutsiia, p. 174.

72.   Lozh' ne k litsu sotsial-demokraticheskoi gazete. [A Lie behind the Back of a Social-Democratic Newspaper.] (Trans. from the Georgian.)

     Unsigned article in Dro, no. 5, Mar. 16, 1907, according to Proletarskaia Revoliutsiia, p. 174.

73.   Nuzhna-li agitatsiia iz Dumy? [Is Duma Agitation Necessary?] (Trans. from the Georgian.)

     Unsigned article in Dro, no. 5, Mar. 16, 1907, according to Proletarskaia Revoliutsiia, p. 174.

74.   Proletariat boretsia, burzhuaziia zakliuchaet soiuz s pravitel'stvom. [The Proletariat Is Fighting, the Bourgeoisie Is Concluding an Alliance with the Government.] (Trans. from the Georgian.)

     Unsigned article in Dro, no. 6, Mar. 17, 1907.

II, 22-26.

75.   Pamiati Tov. G. Teliia. [Comrade G. Telia. In Memoriam.] (Trans. from the Georgian.)

     Article signed "Ko..." in Dro, no. 10, Mar. 22, 1907.

II, 27-31.

76.   Tiflisskaia S.-D. Konferentsiia. [The Tiflis Social-Democratic Conference.] (Trans. from the Georgian.)

     Article signed "Ko..." in Dro, nos. 11, 12, 14, Mar. 23, 24, 27, 1907, according to Proletarskaia Revoliutsiia, p. 174.

77.   Gazeta "Isari" i agrarnyi vopros. [The Newspaper "Isari" and the Agrarian Question.] (Trans. from the Georgian.)

     Article signed "Ko..." in Dro, no. 19, Apr. 1, 1907, according to Proletarskaia Revoliutsiia, p. 174.

78.   Peredovoi proletariat i piatyi s''ezd partii. [The Advanced Proletariat and the Fifth Party Congress.] (Trans. from the Georgian.)

     Unsigned article in Dro, no. 25, Apr. 8, 1907.

II, 32-34.

79. Nerazberikha... [Muddle...] (Trans. from the Georgian.)
    Unsigned article in Dro, no. 26, Apr. 10, 1907.
    II, 38-40.

80. Pochemu Duma bessil'na? [Why Is the Duma Powerless?]
    (Trans. from the Georgian.)
    Unsigned article in Dro, no. 27, Apr. 11, 1907, accord-
    ing to Proletarskaia Revoliutsiia, p. 174.

81. Duma dlia naroda illi narod dlia Dumy? [Is the Duma for the
    People or Are the People for the Duma?] (Trans. from the
    Georgian.)
    Unsigned article in Dro, no. 27, Apr. 11, 1907, accord-
    ing to Proletarskaia Revoliutsiia, p. 174.

82. Nashi kavkazskie klouny. [Our Caucasian Clowns.] (Trans.
    from the Georgian.)
    Unsigned article in Dro, no. 29, Apr. 13, 1907.
    II, 38-40.

83. Statements at Fifth Party Congress.

    First statement, May 10, 1907, in Protokoly, Piatyi
    S''ezd RSDRP (Moscow: Partizdat, 1935) pp. 367-368.

    Second statement, May 10, in Protokoly, p. 368.

84. Razgon Dumy i zadachi proletariata. [The Dispersion of the
    Duma and the Tasks of the Proletariat.]
    Unsigned article in Bakinskii Proletarii, no. 1, June 20,
    1907.
    II, 41-45.

85. Kadetskaia opasnost' i izbiratel'noe soglashenie. [The Kadet
    Danger and the Electoral Agreement.]
    Article in Bakinskii Proletarii no. 2, July 10, 1907,
    according to F. Makharadze, "Pervye pechatnye trudy
    tovarishcha Stalina, " Kniga i Proletarskaia Revoliutsiia,
    1939, no. 12, p. 42.

86. Londonskii s''ezd Rossiiskoi Sotsial-Demokraticheskoi Rabochei Partii (Zapiski delegata). [The London Congress of the
Russian Social-Democratic Labor Party (Notes of a Delegate).]
    Article signed "Koba Ivanovich" in Bakinskii Proletarii,
nos. 1 and 2, June 20 and July 10, 1907.
II, 46-77.

87. Sredi S. -D. [Among the Social-Democrats.]
    Article in Gudok, no. 2, Aug. 22, according to E.
Iaroslavskii, O Tovarishche Staline (Moscow: Gos. izd. pol.
lit., 1941), p. 49.

88. Nakaz Sotsial-Demokraticheskim deputatam III Gosudarstven-
noi Dumy. [Mandate to the Social-Democratic Deputies in the
Third State Duma.]
    Leaflet published in Sept., 1907, subsequent to a meeting
of Sept. 22.
II, 78-80.

89. Nado boikotirovat' soveshchanie! [Boycott the Conference!]
    Article signed "Ko..." in Gudok, no. 4, Sept. 29, 1907.
II, 81-86.

90. Obituary to Khanlar.
    Published in Gudok, no. 5, Oct. 14, 1907, according to
E. Iarsolavskii, O Tovarishche Staline (Moscow: Gos. izd.
pol. lit., 1941), pp. 51-52.

91. Leaflet concerning the murder of Khanlar.
    Attributed to Stalin by E. Iaroslavskii, O Tovarishche
Staline (Moscow: Gos. izd. pol. lit., 1941), pp. 51-52.

1908

92. Pered vyborami. [Before the Elections.]
    Unsigned article in Gudok, no. 14, Jan. 13, 1908.
II, 87-91.

93. Eshche o soveshchanii s garantiiami. [More about a Conference
with Guarantees.]
    Unsigned article in Gudok, no. 14, Jan. 13, 1908.
II, 92-97.

94. Chto govoriat nashi zabastovki poslednego vremeni? [What Do Our Recent Strikes Tell Us?]
    Article signed "K. Kato" in Gudok, no. 21, March 2, 1908
    II, 98-101.

95. Izveshchenie o shtabe samooborony pri Bakinskom Komitete. [Information of the Self-Defense Staff of the Baku Committee.]
    Memo (?) of March 5, 1907, according to Anisimov,
    p. 116, who makes attribution with no explanation of sources.

96. Povorot v taktike neftepromyshlennikov. [The Change in the Oil Owners' Tactics.]
    Unsigned article in Gudok, no. 22, March 9, 1908.
    II, 102-106.

97. Nado gotovit'sia! [We Must Prepare!]
    Unsigned article in Gudok, no. 23, March 16, 1908.
    II, 107-109.

98. Mezhdu prochim. [Among Other Things.]
    Article signed "K. Kato" in Gudok, no. 23, March 16,
    according to Proletarskaia Revoliutsiia, p. 175.

99. Bezgramotnost' ili provokatsiia? [Illiteracy or Provocation?]
    Article signed "K. Kato" in Gudok, no. 23, March 16,
    1908, according to Proletarskaia Revoliutsiia, p. 175.

100. Ekonomicheskii terror i rabochee dvizhenie. [Economic Terrorism and the Labor Movement.]
    Unsigned article in Gudok, no. 25, March 30, 1908.
    II, 110-113.

101. Neftepromyshlenniki ob ekonomicheskom terrore. [The Oil Owners on Economic Terrorism.]
    Article signed "K. Kato" in Gudok, nos. 28, 30, 32,
    dated April 21 and May 4 and 18, 1908.
    II, 114-127.

102.   Klassovaia bor'ba i ekonomicheskii terror. [The Class Struggle and Economic Terrorism.]

       Article in Bakinskii Proletarii, May 15, 1908, according to Makharadze, "Pervye pechatnye trudy tovarishcha Stalina," Kniga i Proletarskaia Revoliutsiia, no. 12, 1939, p. 42.

103.   Pressa. [The Press.]

       Article signed "Ko..." in Bakinskii Proletarii, no. 5, July 20, 1908.

    II, 128-133.

104.   Soveshchanie i rabochie. [The Conference and the Workers.]

       Article signed "Koba" in Bakinskii Proletarii, prilozhenie, no. 5, July 20, 1908.

1909

105.   Partiinyi krizis i nashi zadachi. [The Party Crisis and Our Tasks.]

       Unsigned article in Bakinskii Proletarii, nos. 6 and 7, Aug. 1 and 27, 1909.

    II, 146-158.

106.   K predstoiashchei obshchei zabastovke. [The Forthcoming General Strike.]

       Article signed "K. Ko..." in Bakinskii Proletarii, no. 7, Aug. 27, 1909.

    II, 159-164.

107.   Iz partii. [Party News.]

       Unsigned article dated Aug. 2, 1909, in Bakinskii Proletarii, no. 7, Aug. 27, 1909.

    II, 165-168.

108.   O dekabr'skoi zabastovke i dekabr'skom dogovore. [The December Strike and the December Agreement.]

       Leaflet dated Dec. 13, 1909, signed "Bakinskii Komitet RSDRP."

    II, 169-173.

109. Pis'ma s Kavkaza, I. Baku. II. Tiflis. [Letters from the
      Caucasus. I. Baku. II. Tiflis.]
         Article signed "K.S.," written in Nov.-Dec., 1909 (one
      portion is dated Dec. 20 in manuscript), and published in
      Sotsial-Demokrat*, no. 11, Feb. 13, 1910 (part I) and
      "prilozhenie" entitled "Diskussionnom Listke" of Sotsial-
      Demokrat, no. 2, May 25, 1910 (part II).
      II, 174-197.

                              1910

110. K chitateliu. [To the Reader.]
         Leading article in Tiflisskii Proletarii, no. 1, Jan. 5,
      1910, according to Beria, pp. 189-190, which includes ex-
      cerpts. He indicates that this newspaper appeared in Russian
      and Georgian, but it is not clear which language Stalin wrote
      the original in. Anisimov, p. 116, also attributes this article
      to Stalin on basis of article by I. Nilonov, entitled "Tiflis-
      skii Proletari" in Bibliograficheskii Biuleten' Marksistko-
      Leninskoi Literatury, no. 12, 1939. No information on
      signature.

111. Rezoliutsii priniatye Bakinskim Komitetom 22 ianvaria 1910 g.
      [Resolutions adopted by the Baku Committee, Jan. 22, 1910.]
         Unsigned leaflet.
      II, 197-200.

112. Avgust Bebel', vozhd' germanskikh rabochikh. [August Bebel,
      Leader of the German Workers.]
         Proclamation of Mar. 23, 1910, signed "Bakinskii Komite
      RSDRP."
      II, 201-208.

113. Letter to the Central Committee (from Solvychegodsk).
         Signed "K.S.," dated Dec. 31, 1910. According to
      Trotsky, Stalin* (New York: Harper and Bros., 1941), p.
      133 this letter was first published in fuller form in Zaria
      Vostoka (Tiflis), Dec. 23, 1925, and included greetings to
      Kamenev at the opening. It was again published in B*,
      nos. 1-2, 1932, pp. 10-13.
      II, 209-212.

1911

114. Letter to V.S. Bobrovskii (from Sovychegodsk).
According to Trotsky, Stalin (New York: Harper and Bros.,
1941), p. 133, this letter of Jan. 24, 1911, was published
along with preceding entry in Zaria Vostoka, Dec. 23, 1925,
but the present entry--unlike the other--was entirely suppressed afterwards. See excerpts (in English) in Trotsky's
book, pp. 130-131. The existence of the letter is confirmed
and excerpts of the Russian text are published in M. Mos-
kalev, Russkoe biuro TsK bol'shevistskoi partii 1912-1917
(Moscow, 1947), p. 31, and by P. Pospelov, Pravda, Jan. 18, 1962.

115. Iz lageria Stolypinskoi "rabochei" partii. [From the Camp of
the Stolypin "Workers."]
Article signed "K" in Sotsial-Demokrat*, no. 23, Sept. 1,
1911. At this time it is questionable that this signature indicates Stalin's authorship, though Beria, p. 199, attributes
it to Stalin and quotes from Lenin's approving comment on it
in his Sochineniia, 4th ed., XV, p. 217.

116. Proclamation.
According to Beria, pp. 200-205, Stalin "wrote" a proclamation, which Beria quotes in what purports to be full form,
signed "Rukov. kruzh. Tifl. gruppy RSDRP." He also quotes
pp. 205-206, a comment on this proclamation in Sotsial-
Demokrat, no. 24, Oct. 18, 1911, which refers to the item
as just published, thus placing the date of publication of the
proclamation around mid-October. The content of the proclamation is inconclusive in determining authorship, but the
circumstances lead one to doubt that Stalin wrote it. At no
time in 1911 was he in or near the Caucasus although it is
not inconceivable that he wrote this proclamation in Solvychegodsk, Vologda or St. Petersburg and dispatched it for
publication in Tiflis.

1912

117. Za partiiu! [For the Party!]
Proclamation of March 1912, signed "Tsentral'nyi Komi-
tet RSDRP."
II, 213-218.

118. Da zdravstvuet Pervoe Maia! [Long Live the First of May!]
         Proclamation issued in April 1912, signed "Tsentral'nyi
     Komitet RSDRP."
     II, 219-224.

119. Novaia polosa. [A New Period.]
         Article signed "K.S." Zvezda, no. 30, April 15, 1912.
     II, 225-226.

120. Liberal'nye farisei. [Liberal Hypocrites.]
         Article signed "S." in Zvezda, no. 30, April 15, 1912.
     II, 227-228.

121. Bespartiinye chudaki. [Non-Party Simpletons.]
         Article signed "K.S.--n" in Zvezda, no. 30, April 15,
     1912.
     II, 229-231.

122. Zhizn' pobezhdaet! [Life Triumphs!]
         Article signed "K. Solin" in Zvezda, no. 30, April 15,
     1912.
     II, 232-233.

123. Oni khorosho rabotaiut... [They Are Working Well...]
         Article signed "K. Solin" in Zvezda, no. 31, April 17,
     1912.
     II, 234-236.

124. Tronulas'! ... [The Ice Has Broken! ...]
         Article signed "K.S." in Zvezda, no. 32, April 19, 1912.
     II, 237-239.

125. Kak oni gotoviatsia k vyboram. [How They Are Preparing for
     the Elections.]
         Article signed "K. Solin" in Zvezda, no. 32, April 19,
     1912.
     II, 240-243.

126. Vyvody. [Deductions.]
         Article signed "K. Solin" in Zvezda, no. 33, April 22,
      1912.
      II, 244-247.

127. Nashi tseli. [Our Aims.]
         Unsigned article in P*, no. 1, April 22, 1912.
      II, 248-249.

128. Nakaz peterburgskikh rabochikh svoemu rabochemu deputatu.
      [Mandate of the St. Petersburg Workers to Their Labor
      Deputy.]
         Unsigned leaflet from first half of Oct., 1912.
      II, 250-252.

129. Kto pobedil? [Who Won?]
         Unsigned article in P, no. 146, Oct. 18, 1912, according
      to Bol'shevistskaia "Pravda," K 25-letiiu osnovaniia
      "Pravda" (Moscow: Partizdat, 1937), pp. 176-177, without
      any explanation of this attribution.

130. Volia upolnomochennykh. [The Will of the Voters' Delegates.]
         Article signed "K. St." in P* no. 147, Oct. 19, 1912.
      II, 253-255.

131. K itogam vyborov po rabochei kurii Peterburga. [The Results
      of the Elections in the Workers' Curia of St. Petersburg.]
         Article signed "K. St." in P*, no. 151, Oct. 24, 1912.
      II, 256-261.

132. Segodnia vybory. [Today Is Election Day.]
         Article signed "K. St." in P*, no. 152, Oct. 25, 1912.
      II, 262-265.

133. Letter to Editor of Sotsial-Demokrat.
         Photographic facsimile of handwritten, damaged note of
      Oct. 29 or 30, 1912, published in Bol'shevistskaia "Pravda,"
      K 25-letiu osnovaniia "Pravada"* (Moscow: Partizdat, 1937),
      pp. 168-169.

134. Iagello kak nepolnopravnyi chlen' s.-d. fraktsii. [Iagello as a
      Limited Member of the S.-D. Duma Group.]
         Article signed "K. Stalin" in P*, no. 182, Dec. 1, 1912.

135. Ko vsem rabochim i rabotnitsam Rossii! [To All the Working
      Men and Working Women of Russia!]
         Leaflet in name of Central Committee published end of
         Dec. 1912, or early Jan. 1913.
      II, 266-270.

                              1913

136. Fakticheskaia spravka. [A Factual Reference.]
         Article signed "K. Stalin" in Prosveshchenie*, no. 1,
         Jan., 1913, pp. 80-82.

137. Vybory v Peterburge. [The Elections in St. Petersburg.]
         Article signed "K. Stalin" in Sotsial-Demokrat*, no. 30,
         Jan. 12, 1913.
      II, 271-284.

138. Na puti k natsionalizmu. [On the Road to Nationalism.]
         Article signed "K. St." in Sotsial-Demokrat*, no. 30,
         Jan. 12, 1913.
      II, 285-289.

139. Marksizm i natsional'nyi vopros. [Marxism and the National
      Question.]
         Article signed "K. Stalin, Vienna, January, 1913" in
         Prosveshchenie*, nos. 3-5, March (pp. 50-62), April (pp. 22-
         41) and May (pp. 25-36), 1913. Originally entitled "Natsional
         vopros i Sotsial-Demokratii" ("The National Question and
         the Social-Democratic Party"). In the original version the
         following appeared and should appear in Sochineniia, II, 312,
         following line 9: "Togda natsional'naia bor'ba, uidia iz politik
         zamknetsia v khoziaistvennuiu sferu, gde ona budet ograni-
         chivatsia konkurentsiei tovaroprodavtsev do samago kontsa
         kapitalizma. No takaia bor'ba ne zadevaet priamo rabochikh
         i ne predstavliaet dlia nikh ser'eznoi opasnosti." The follow-
         ing passage also appeared in the original and was omitted

from S̲, II, 353, where it should follow line 8: "V vidu etogo my ochen' somnevaemsia v uspekhakh organizatsionnago federalizma na Kavkaze." These changes and a number of less significant alterations were made considerably before it was published in 1946 and therefore do not reflect the work of the S̲ editors. In the case of the first omission noted above, the editor responsible for the excision of this highly optimistic affirmation is the anonymous one who prepared the essay for republication as a separate booklet, entitled "Natsional'nyi vopros i marksizm" ("The National Question and Marxism") in 1914.

There has been considerable discussion of the authorship of this article. Trotsky in his Stalin (New York: Harpers, 1941), pp. 156-158, asserted that Lenin was really its principal author, a view sustained by Bertram Wolfe and Isaac Deutscher in their biographical works on Stalin. On the other hand, Richard Pipes in The Formation of the Soviet Union (Cambridge: Harvard, 1954), pp. 40-41, and the present writer in "Trotsky's Interpretation of Stalin," Canadian Slavonic Papers V, p. 90, have disagreed. Milovan Djilas, in his Conversations with Stalin (New York: Harcourt, Brace and World, 1962), p. 157, recollects that Stalin said of his essay "That was Ilyich's-Lenin's view. Ilyich also edited the book." The context of this statement makes it unclear whether the "view" was the entire essay or one particular question under discussion in Djilas' presence. It also fails to clarify the kind of influence Lenin exercised on the essay. Stalin may have been referring to conversations he is known to have had with Lenin on the nationality problem just before writing the essay in Vienna (while Lenin stayed in Cracow), or he may have been referring to some work performed by Lenin after Stalin signed the essay in Vienna but before it was published in Petersburg. However, the use of the word "book"(in Michael Petrovich's translation from the Serbo-Croatian) indicates to this writer that Stalin is referring to the republication of the three article-size installments of 1913 in the one small book (or booklet) of 1914, noted above. One can readily imagine Lenin taking charge of the republication of the work in "book" form, considering his interest in the topic at this time, and the "editing" referred to by Stalin probably consists of the changing of the title, various stylistic modifications that a comparison of the 1913 and 1914 texts reveals, and the substantive change (S̲, II, 312) noted above. On balance it is this student's conclusion that Lenin certainly helped form Stalin's ideas on the nationality question before the essay of 1913 was composed, and Lenin probably edited it for republi-

cation in 1914 (his changes being retained in all later versions), but that the work remains essentially Stalin's.
II, 290-367.

140. Polozhenie v Sotsial-Demokraticheskoi fraktsii. [The Situation
in the Social-Democratic Group in the Duma.]
        Article signed "K. Stalin" in P* no. 47, Feb. 26, 1913.
II, 368-372.

141. Godovshchina Lenskoi boini. [The Anniversary of the Lena
Massacre.]
        Leaflet written in Jan.-Feb., 1913 in name of Central
Committee.
II, 373-376.

1915

142. Letter to Lenin, Feb. 27, 1915.
        Photocopy in Proletarskaia Revoliutsiia*, no. 7, 1936,
p. 168. Signed "Vash Koba."

143. Letter to A.S. Alliluev, Nov. 25, 1915.
        In A.S. Alliluev, Iz vospominanii* (Moscow: Izd. Pravda
1946), p. 21.

1916

144. Letter to editor of Voprosy strakhovaniia, March 12, 1916.
        Signed by "I. Dzhugashvili" and Vladkin, Maslennikov,
Medvedev, Pivon, Spandarian and Shveitser; published in
Proletarskaia Revoliutsiia*, no. 7, 1936, p. 168.

1917

145. O Sovdepakh Rabochikh i Soldatskikh Deputatov. [The Soviet of
Workers' and Soldiers' Deputies.]
        Article signed "K. Stalin." in P*, March 14, 1917.
III, 1-3.

146. O voine. [The War.]
Article signed "K. Stalin" in P*, March 16, 1917.
III, 4-8.

147. Na puti k ministerskim portfeliam. [Bidding for Ministerial
Portfolios.]
Articles signed "K. Stalin" in P*, March 17, 1917. Ori-
ginally the group seeking portfolios was referred to as the
"Bur'ianovskii" group; to this "Plekhanovskii" has been
hyphenated (p. 9).
III, 9-10.

148. Ob usloviiakh pobedy russkoi revoliutsii. [Conditions for the
Victory of the Russian Revolution.]
Article signed "K. Stalin" in P*, March 18, 1917.
III, 11-15.

149. Ob otmene natsional'nykh ogranichenii. [Abolition of National
Disabilities.]
Article signed "K. Stalin" in P*, March 25, 1917.
III, 16-19.

150. Ili--ili. [Either--or.]
Unsigned article in P*, March 26, 1917.
III, 20-22.

151. Protiv federalizma. [Against Federalism.]
Article signed "K. Stalin" in P*, March 28, 1917. "Primechanie avtora," which follows this in S, III, 28-31, dated
Dec., 1924, is transplanted from "Oktiabr'skaia revoliutsiia
i taktika russkikh kommunistov," which is the preface to an
anthology of writings by Stalin in 1917. See below, No. 662.
III, 23-28.

152. Report to Petrograd Party Conference, March 29, 1917.
Stenographic version in Trotsky, Stalinskaia shkola
fal'shivikatsii (Berlin: Izdatel'stvo "Granit," 1932), pp. 231-
232. Verified and summarized on basis of archives in USSR
in F.I. Drabkina, "Vserossiiskoe soveshchanie bol'shevikov
v marte 1917 goda," Voprosy Istorii, no. 9, 1956, pp. 9-11.

153.　Dve rezoliutsii. [Two Resolutions.]
　　　　　Article signed "K. Stalin" in P*, April 11, 1917.
　　　III, 32-33.

154.　Zemliu--krest'ianam. [The Land to the Peasants.]
　　　　　Article signed "K. Stalin" in P*, April 11, 1917.
　　　III, 34-36.

155.　Pervoe Maia. [May Day.]
　　　　　Unsigned article in P*, April 18, 1917.
　　　III, 37-38.

156.　O vremennom pravitel'stve. [The Provisional Government.]
　　　　　Speech of April 18, 1917, signed and published in Soldat-
　　　skaia Pravda, April 25, 1917.
　　　III, 39-42.

157.　O soveshchanii v Mariinskom Dvortse. [The Conference in the
　　　Mariinskii Palace.]
　　　　　Article signed "K. Stalin" in P*, April 25, 1917.
　　　III, 43-47.

158.　Statements in April Conference of Party, April 24-29, 1917.

　　　　　Statement in support of Lenin, April 24.
　　　III, 48-49.

　　　　　Report on the National Question, April 29.
　　　III, 49-55.

　　　　　Conclusion on the National Question, April 29.
　　　III, 29.

　　　　　All appeared in Petrogradskaia Obshchegorodskaia i
　　　Vserossiiskaia Konferentsiia RSKRP (b)* (Moscow-Leningrad:
　　　Gosizdat, 1925).

159.　Otstavshie ot revoliutsii. [Lagging behind the Revolution.]
　　　　　Article signed "K. Stalin" in P*, May 4, 1917.
　　　III, 58-63.

160.   Ispravlenie oshibki. [A Correction of a Mistake.]
            Signed note in P*, May 5, 1917.

161.   Chego my zhdali ot konferentsii? [What Did We Expect from
        the Conference?]
            Article signed "K. Stalin" in Soldatskaia Pravda, May 6,
            1917.
        III, 67-69.

162.   Comment in closed session of Petrograd Committee of the
        Party, May 10, 1917.
            In Pervyi legal'nyi peterburgskii komitet Bol'shevikov v
            1917 g.* (Moscow: Giz, 1927), pp. 98-99.

163.   Munitsipal'naia kampaniia. [The Municipal Election Campaign.]
            Article signed "K. Stalin" in P*, May 21, 24, 26, 1917.
        III, 67-69.

164.   Statement in closed session of Petrograd Committee of the
        Party, June 6, 1917.
            In Pervyi legal'nyi peterburgskii komitet Bol'shevikov v
            1917 g.* (Moscow: Giz, 1927), p. 141.

165.   Vchera i segodnia. [Yesterday and Today.]
            Article signed "K. Stalin" in Soldatskaia Pravda, June 13,
            1917.
        III, 80-87.

166.   Protiv razroznennykh demonstratsii. [Against Isolated Demon-
        strations.]
            Article signed "K. Stalin" in P*, June 14, 1917.
        III, 88-90.

167.   K itogam munitsipal'nykh vyborov v Petrograde. [Results of
        the Petrograd Municipal Elections.]
            Article signed "K. Stalin" in Biulleteni Biuro Pechati pri
            TsK RSDRP, June 15, 1917.
        III, 91-95.

168.   Ko vsem trudiashchimsia, ko vsem rabochim i soldatam Petro
       grada. [To All the Toilers, to All the Workers and Soldiers of
       Petrograd.]
              Proclamation P*, June 17, 1917, signed by various Party
       bodies.
       III, 96-99.

169.   Na demonstratsii. [At the Demonstration.]
              Article signed "K. St." in P*, June 20, 1917. The follow
       ing sentence, possibly qualifying the political meaning of the
       article, is omitted from p. 101, line 4: "A obyvatel', za-
       pugannyi, dolzhno byt', tragikomicheskimi prizyvami
       'voennoi ligi', predpochel izdali sledit' za demonstratsiei."
       III, 100-103.

170.   Report to All-Russian Bolshevik Military Conference, June 17,
       1917.
              Synopsis of report, partly in direct quotation, in Novaia
       Zhizn'*, June 22, 1917.

171.   Smykaite riady! [Close the Ranks!]
              Article signed "K. Stalin" in Proletarskoe Delo, July 15,
       1917.
       III, 104-107.

172.   Statements at Petrograd Party Conference, July 16-20, 1917.

              Central Committee Report on July Events, July 16.
       III, 108-114.

              Report on the Current Situation, July 16. Omits following
       passage, which should follow last line of page 121: "... 5-go
       iiulia, kogda Tsentral'nyi Komitet nashei partii prizyval
       likvidirovat' demonstratsii, ia na zasendanii Tsentral'nogo
       Ispolnitel'nogo Komiteta skazal kontr-revoliutsiia idet, ona
       dushit nas, no sleduiushchaia ochered' za vami, daite nam
       ruku dlia bor'by s kontr-revoliutsiei. Kogda eto predlozhenie
       my snesli na Plenum, nas osmeiali: kakoe mozhet byt'
       edinstvo s liud'mi, zapiatnavshimi [sic] sebia krov'iu i
       shpionazhem. 6-go i 7-go iiulia okonchatel'no vyiasnilos',
       chto men'sheviki i s.-r-y protiv nas, v soiuze s kontr-revo-
       liutsiei. Teper', my dolzhny samym reshitel'nym obrazom
       otvergat' skhemu edineniia s soiuznikami kontr-revoliutsii,

u kotorykh ruki v krovi rabochikh i soldat. Tem, men'she-
vikam i s.-r-am, kotorye khotiat borot'sia s kontr-revo-
liutsiei, my dolzhny pomogat' otorvat'sia ot oborontsev,
izmennikov revoliutsii. Ia predlagaiu vam skhemu ob'edineniia levogo flanga revoliutsii."
III, 122-123.

Answers to questions, July 16.
III, 122-123.

Conclusion, July 16.
III, 123-126.

All appeared in Krasnaia Letopis'*, no. 7, 1923.

173.   Kontrrevoliutsiia shturmuet, oborontsy khoroniat revoliutsiiu.
(The Counterrevolution Attacks, the Defenders Bury the Revolution.)
Unsigned article in Rabochii i Soldat, July 17, 1917,
according to Stalin anthology Na putiakh k Oktiabriu* (Moscow: Giz, 1925), pp. 99-101, which reprints it.

174.   Chto sluchilos'? [What Has Happened?]
Unsigned article in Rabochii i Soldat*, July 23, 1917.
III, 127-129.

175.   Pobeda kontrrevoliutsii. [Victory of the Counterrevolution.]
Article signed "K. St." in Rabochii i Soldat*, July 23,
1917.
III, 130-133.

176.   V chem nasha sila? [In What Lies Our Strength?]
Unsigned article in Rabochii i Soldat*, July 23, 1917,
attributed to Stalin by editors of the official reprint of Pravda:
Bol'shevistskaia Pravda* (Leningrad: Priboi, 1929), vyp.
no. 1, pp. 1-2. The entire article is reproduced here. This
republication was in general a seriou scholarly undertaking
and utilized careful research into the authorship of unsigned
and pseudonymous articles, interviewing persons who might
have been authors.

177.   Pobeda kadetov. [The Victory of the Kadets.]
            Unsigned article in Rabochii i Soldat*, July 24, 1917.
        III, 134-136.

178.   Ko vsem trudiashchimsia, ko vsem rabochim i soldatam Petro-
        grada. [To All the Toilers, to All the Workers and Soldiers of
        Petrograd.]
            Proclamation signed by Petrograd Bolshevik Conference
        in Rabochii i Soldat*, July 24, 1917.
        III, 137-143.

179.   Dve konferentsii. [Two Conferences.]
            Unsigned article in Rabochii i Soldat*, July 24, 1917.
        III, 144-145.

180.   Novoe pravitel'stvo. [The New Government.]
            Unsigned article in Rabochii i Soldat*, July 26, 1917.
        III, 146-148.

181.   K vyboram v uchreditel'noe sobranie. [The Constituent Assem-
        bly Elections.]
            Article signed "K. Stalin" in Rabochii i Soldat*, July 27,
        1917.
        III, 149-155.

182.   Statements at Sixth Party Congress, July 26 – Aug. 3, 1917.

            Central Committee report, July 27.
        III, 156-168.

            Conclusion on report, July 27.
        III, 168-170.

            Procedural proposal, July 27. Protokoly s''ezdov i kon-
        ferentsii VKP(b): Shestoi s''ezd* (Moscow: Istpart, 1927),
        p. 30.

            Report on the political situation, July 30.
        III, 171-178.

            Replies to questions on the report, July 31.
        III, 182-186.

Conclusion on the report, July 31.
III, 182-186.

Remarks in discussion of resolution, Aug. 3. Discussion
of the various versions of this material is complicated by
the fact that no official stenographic report was recorded
during the congress itself. However, several witnesses put
down their recollected versions of the meeting, which were
published in 1919: Protokoly VI s"ezda RSDRP(b) 26 iiulia-
3 avgusta 1917 g.* (Moscow and Petrograd: Izd. Kommunist,
1919); in 1927 this version was republished. In 1934 an
attempt at a more definitive edition was made, utilizing contemporary newspaper reports and the newly found, private
record by Kozlov. See Shestoi s"ezd RSDRP(b)* (Moscow:
IMEL, 1934). Then in compiling Stalin's Sochineniia a new
version of his contributions to the congress was devised,
utilizing the 1919 edition and some contemporary newspapers,
but not as much material as was used for the 1934 edition, it
seems. In particular the 1934 edition, while omitting some
portions of Stalin's speeches of July 27 and 30, includes
other material not in the S version of these speeches. Also,
S includes only a small portion of Stalin's numerous comments on the draft resolution (Aug. 3); others occur scattered
through pp. 228-234 of the 1934 edition. Finally, S excludes
a short procedural proposal by Stalin (July 27).
Excerpt: III, 186-187.

183. Chego khotiat kapitalisty? [What Do the Capitalists Want?]
      Unsigned article in Rabochii i Soldat*, Aug. 6, 1917.
   III, 188-192.

184. Protiv moskovskogo soveshchaniia. [Against the Moscow Conference.]
      Unsigned article in Rabochii i Soldat*, Aug. 8, 1917.
   III, 193-195.

185. Eshche o Stokgol'me. [More on the Subject of Stockholm.]
      Unsigned article in Rabochii i Soldat*, Aug. 9, 1917.
   III, 196-199.

186. Kuda vedet moskovskoge soveshchanie? [Whither the Moscow
   Conference?]
      Unsigned article in Proletarii*, Aug. 13, 1917.
   III, 200-205.

187.   Kontrrevoliutsiia i narody Rossii. [Counterrevolution and
         the Peoples of Russia.]
              Unsigned article in Proletarii*, Aug. 13, 1917.
         III, 206-209.

188.   Dva puti. [Two Courses.]
              Unsigned article in Proletarii*, Aug. 15, 1917.
         III, 210-213.

189.   Itogi moskovskogo soveshchaniia. [Outcome of the Moscow
         Conference.]
              Unsigned article in Proletarii*, 214-215.
         III, 214-216.

190.   Pravda o nashem porazhenii na fronte. [The Truth About Our
         Defeat at the Front.]
              Unsigned article in Proletarii*, Aug. 18, 1917.
         III, 217-220.

191.   O prichinakh iiul'skogo porazheniia na fronte. [The Cause of
         the July Defeat at the Front.]
              Unsigned article in Proletarii*, Aug. 18, 1917.
         III, 221-226.

192.   Kto zhe vinovat v porazhenii na fronte? [Who Really Is Respon-
         sible for the Defeat at the Front?]
              Article signed "K. Stalin" in brochure "Kto vinovat v
         porazhenii na fronte" (Petrograd: Priboi, 1917), which
         consists of this article and one by Zinoviev on the same
         general topic, which is not noted in S. Zinoviev's article
         appears in his Sochineniia, vol. VII (1), pp. 271-285.
         III, 227-231.

193.   Amerikanskie milliardy. [American Billions.]
              Unsigned article in Proletarii*, Aug. 19, 1917.
         III, 231-235.

194.   Segodnia vybory. [This Is Election Day.]
              Unsigned article in Proletarii*, Aug. 20, 1917.
         III, 236-240.

195.   Polosa provokatsii. [A Period of Provocation.]
             Unsigned article in Proletarii*, Aug. 22, 1917.
         III, 241-243.

196.   Razdelenie truda v partii "Sotsialistov-revoliutsionerov."
         [Division of Labor in the "Socialist Revolutionary" Party.]
             Unsigned article in Proletarii*, Aug. 23, 1917.
         III, 244-247.

197.   Soiuz zheltykh. [Yellow Alliance.]
             Unsigned article in Proletarii*, Aug. 25, 1917.
         III, 248-250.

198.   Ili--ili. [Either--Or.]
             Unsigned article in Rabochii*, Aug. 25, 1917.
         III, 251-255.

199.   My trebuem! [We Demand!]
             Unsigned article in Rabochii*, Aug. 28, 1917.
         III, 256-260.

200.   Zagovor prodolzhaetsia. [The Conspiracy Continues.]
             Unsigned article in Rabochii*, Aug. 28, 1917.
         III, 261-265.

201.   Protiv soglashenii s burzhuaziei. [Against Compromise with
         the Bourgeoisie.]
             Unsigned article in Rabochii*, Aug. 31, 1917. The words
         "s burzhuaziei" in the title do not occur in the original ver-
         sion.
         III, 266-267.

202.   Krizis i direktoriia. [The Crisis and the Directory.]
             Unsigned article in Rabochii Put'*, Sept. 3, 1917.
         III, 268-271.

203.   Svoim putem. [They Will Not Swerve from Their Path.]
             Unsigned article in Rabochii Put'*, Sept. 6, 1917.
         III, 272-274.

204.   O razryve s Kadetami. [The Break with the Kadets.]
            Article signed "K. St." in Rabochii Put'*, Sept. 6,
        1917.
        III, 275-278.

205.   Vtoraia volna. [The Second Wave.]
            Article signed "K. Stalin" in Rabochii Put', Sept. 9, 1917
        III, 279-285.

206.   Inostrantsy i zagovor Kornilova. [Foreigners and the Kornilov
        Conspiracy.]
            Article signed "K." in Rabochii Put'*, Sept. 12, 1917.

207.   K demokraticheskomu soveshchaniiu. [The Democratic Confer-
        ence.]
            Unsigned article in Rabochii Put'*, Sept. 14, 1917.
        III, 289-293.

208.   Dve linii. [Two Lines.]
            Unsigned article in Rabochii Put'*, Sept. 16, 1917.
        III, 294-296.

209.   Vsia vlast' sovetam! [All Power to the Soviets!]
            Unsigned article in Rabochii Put'*, Sept. 27, 1917.
        III, 294-299.

210.   O revoliutsionnom fronte. [The Revolutionary Front.]
            Unsigned article in Rabochii Put'*, Sept. 19, 1917.
        III, 300-304.

211.   Kuiut tsepi. [Forging Chains.]
            Unsigned article in Rabochii Put'*, Sept. 24, 1917.
        III, 305-308.

212.   Pravitel'stvo burzhuaznoi diktatury. [A Government of
        Bourgeois Dictatorship.]
            Unsigned article in Rabochii Put'*, Sept. 27, 1917.
        III, 309-312.

213.   Otkliki. [Comments.]
            Unsigned article in Rabochii Put'*, Sept. 27, 1917.
        III, 313-316.

214.   Pokhod protiv rabochikh. [Campaign against the Workers.]
            Unsigned article in Rabochii Put'*, Sept. 28, 1917.
        III, 317-319.

215.   Zhdat' vam--ne dozhdat'sia! [You Will Wait in Vain!]
            Unsigned article in Rabochii Put'*, Sept. 29, 1917.
        III, 320-232.

216.   Otkliki. [Comments.]
            Unsigned article in Rabochii Put'*, Sept. 29, 1917.
        III, 324-327.

217.   Bumazhnaia koalitsiia. [A Paper Coalition.]
            Unsigned article in Rabochii Put'*, Sept. 30, 1917.
        III, 328-330.

218.   Otkliki. [Comments.]
            Unsigned article in Rabochii Put'*, Oct. 3, 1917.
        III, 331-334.

219.   Vyselki sebia. [Self-Chastisement.]
            Unsigned article in Rabochii Put'*, Oct. 4, 1917.
        III, 335-336.

220.   Zagovor protiv revoliutsii. [The Plot against the Revolution.]
            Article signed "K. Stalin" in Rabochii Put'*, Oct. 4, 5, 7.
        III, 337-357.

221.   Kto sryvaet uchreditel'noe sobranie? [Who Is Torpedoing the
        Constituent Assembly?]
            Unsigned article in Rabochii Put'*, Oct. 5, 1917.
        III, 358-360.

222. Kontrrevoliutsiia mobilizuetsia--gotovtes' k otporu. [The Counterrevolution Is Mobilizing--Prepare to Resist.]
    Unsigned article in Rabochii Put'*, Oct. 10, 1917.
    III, 361-363

223. Komu nuzhen predparlament? [Who Needs the Preparliament?]
    Unsigned article in Rabochii Put'*, Oct. 10, 1917.
    III, 364-366.

224. Vlast' sovetov. [Soviet Power.]
    Unsigned article in Rabochii Put'*, Oct. 13, 1917.
    III, 367-370.

225. Ekzamen naglosti. [A Study in Brazenness.]
    Unsigned article in Rabochii Put'*, Oct. 15, 1917.
    III, 371-374.

226. Shtreikbrekhery revoliutsii. [Blacklegs of the Revolution.]
    Unsigned article in Rabochii Put'*, Oct. 15, 1917.
    III, 375-380.

227. Speech in Central Committee, Oct. 16, 1917.
    See appendix "A, " containing full list of Stalin's recorded, published statements in the Central Committee.

228. Editorial note to letter from Zinoviev concerning Lenin's letter of Oct. 19 to Central Committee.
    Rabochii Put', Oct. 20, 1917. Unsigned note "ot redaktsii" attributed to Stalin by editors of Pravda No. – No. 1-227 1917 (Moscow, Partizdat, 1932), vyp. VI. This scholarly republication indicates that Stalin acknowledged authorship of this note upon inquiry by the editors of the project.

229. "Okruzhili mia tel'tsy mnozi tuchny." ["Strong Bulls of Bashan Have Beset Me Round."]
    Unsigned article in Rabochii Put'*, Oct. 20, 1917.
    III, 383-386.

230.   Chto nam nuzhno? [What Do We Need?]
       Unsigned article in Rabochii Put'*, Oct. 24, 1917.
       III, 387-390.

231.   Ul'timatum bol'shinstva Ts K RSDRP(b) men'shinstvu. [Ulti-
       matum of the Majority of the C(entral) C(ommittee) of the
       RSDLP(b) to the Minority.]
       Joint statement signed by Lenin, Trotsky, Stalin, Sverd-
       lov, Uritskii, Dzerzhinskii, Ioffe, Bubnov, Sokol'nikov and
       Muranov (thus not to be regarded as especially Stalin's
       work) in Protokoly tsentral'nogo komiteta RSDRP(b). Avgust
       1917--Fevral' 1918* (Moscow, Gos. izd. polit. lit., 1958),
       pp. 133-134.

232.   Deklaratsiia prav narodov Rossii. [Declaration of Rights of
       the Peoples of Russia.]
       Proclamation dated Nov. 2, 1917, published in P*,
       Nov. 3, 1917. Signed by Lenin and "Iosif Dzhugashvili-
       Stalin" but not attributed to Stalin by S, despite the historic
       significance and Bolshevik orthodoxy of this document. How-
       ever, Lenin's Sochineniia does not attribute it to Lenin,
       either. A number of Stalin-era scholarly works do, however,
       attribute it to Stalin. See: Stalin, Stat'i i rechi ob Ukraine.
       Sbornik (Kiev, Izd. Ts. K. KP(b) U, 1936), pp. 12-13;
       bibliographies in Proletarskaia Revoliutsiia, no. 4, 1939,
       p. 180, and Kniga i Proletarskaia Revoliutsiia, no. 12,
       1939, p. 133; and E.I. Pesikina, Narodnyi komissariat po
       delam natsional'nostei i ego deiatel'nost' v 1917-1918 gg.
       (Moscow, 1950), p. 23. It may be added that Stalin's com-
       missariat at this time had almost no staff, and it is very
       likely that official documents emenating from it would have
       been his own work in considerable measure. Why S does not
       attribute the work to him remains a puzzle to this investigator.

233.   Teletype conversation with General Staff, Nov. 9, 1917.
       Message signed by Lenin, Stalin and Krylenko in Lenin,
       published in I, Nov. 10, 1917, and included in Lenin's
       Sochineniia* (3rd ed.), XXII, pp. 69-71. Hence, presumably
       mainly attributable to Lenin.

234.   O natsional'nykh relikviiakh Ukrainy. [The National Relics of
       the Ukraine.]
       Proclamation signed "I. Dzhugashvili-Stalin" in P*,
       Nov. 14, 1917.

235.   Speech to Congress of Finnish Social-Democratic Party,
        Nov. 14, 1917.
                In P*, Nov. 16, 1917.
        IV, 1-5.

236.   Teletype conversation with Porsh and Bakinskii, Nov. 17, 1917.
                Presumably full version, identifying Stalin clearly, is in
        V. Manilov (ed.) 1917 god v kievshchine. Khronika sobytii*
        (Kiev, Partizdat, 1936), I, pp. 531-534. Version in Stalin,
        Stat'i i rechi ob Ukraine (Kiev, Izd. Ts.K. KP(b)U, 1936)
        pp. 14-17, is taken from P, Nov. 24, 1917, and is incom-
        plete.

237.   Note to Lenin, Nov. 19, 1917.
                Signed "I. Stalin, " published in LS*, XXXV, p. 8.

238.   Ko vsem trudiashchimsia musul'manam Rossii i Vostoka.
        [To All Moslem Toilers of Russia and the East.]
                Proclamation signed by Lenin and "Dzhugashvili-Stalin."
        in P*, Nov. 22, 1917. In general the discussion concerning
        No. 232 applies here since the Sochineniia of neither signa-
        tory attributes it to the leader it is treating. Again the topic
        and the circumstances suggest that Stalin played some role
        in the writing of the document, and again the bibliographies
        in Kniga i Proletarskaia Revoliutsiia, no. 12, 1934, p. 133,
        and Proletarskaia Revoliutsiia, p. 180, attributes it to him.

239.   Notes amplifying Lenin's draft of peace terms with Ukraine,
        dated Nov. 27, 1917.
                Published and definitely attributed to Stalin in LS*, XI,
        16.

240.   Declaration on allegations in Petrogradskii Golos.
                Note signed "Dzhugashvili-Stalin" in P*, Dec. 1, 1917.

241.   Certification of S. Shaumian as Commissar of Caucasian
        Affairs, Dec. 5, 1917.
                Signed "Dzhugashvili-Stalin, " published in E. Burdzhalov,
        Dvadtsat' shest' bakinskikh komissarov* (Moscow, Gos. izd.
        pol. lit., 1938), p. 29.

242. Decree on Koran of Osman, Dec. 6, 1917.
           Signed by Lenin and "I. Dzhugashvili-Stalin," published
      in LS*, XXXV, 10. Addressee of this two-word order un-
      clear. Editorial note in LS states that it is in Stalin's hand.

243. General'nyi sekretariat rady i kadetsko-kaledinskaia kontrrevo-
      liutsiia. [The General Secretariat of the Rada and the Kadet-
      Kaledinite Counterrevolution.]
           Article signed "I. Dzugashvili-Stalin" in P*, Dec. 8,
      1917, which appeared in I on the same date under title
      "Ukrainskaia burzhuaziia i kontrrevoliutsiia."

244. Otvet ukrainskim tovarishcham v tylu i na fronte. [Reply to
      UKrainian Comrades in the Rear and at the Front.]
           Article signed "I. Dzhugashvili-Stalin" in P*, Dec. 12,
      1917. On p. 9 first two lines should read: "politicheskoi
      zhizni nashei strany, v rode, okazhem, Soedinennykh
      Shtatov Rossii, esli etogo protrebuet trudovoe naselenie..."
      On p. 13 derogatory references to the Cossacks in lines 6
      and 12 have been changed to refer to Kaledin.

245. Ob ukrainskom rade. [The Ukrainian Rada.]
           Speech of Dec. 14, 1917, published in I*, Dec. 17, 1917.
      IV, 15-18.

246. Chto takoe ukrainskaia rada? [What Is the Ukrainian Rada?]
           Article signed "I. Stalin" in P*, Dec. 15, 1917.
      IV, 19-21.

247. Receipt for funds, Dec. 18, 1917.
           Signed "I. Stalin," published in LS*, XXXV, 11.

248. Draft decree on release of arrested members of the "League
      for the Defense of the Constituent Assembly," Dec. 19, 1917.
           Signed by Lenin and "Stalin," published in LS*, XXI, iii.

249. Speech to Soviet on Finnish independence, Dec. 22, 1917.
           In P*, Dec. 23. On p. 22 the text of the official resolution
      did not appear in the original. P. 23, lines 21-22 should

read "...v kartinu zavoevaniia Finliandiei na nezavisimosti, to my..." P. 24, last para. should read: "Pust' zhe svobod Finliandii dast, v kontse kontsov, polnuiu nezavisimost' rabochikh i krest'ian Finliandii i sozdast prochnuiu bazu druzhby nashikh narodov. "

250. Statement on Cossacks, Dec. 28 or 29, 1917.
    Reply to questions raised by visiting representatives of Don region, included in article headed "Miatezh kontrrevoliutsionnykh generalov" in I*, Dec. 29, 1917.

251. Decree on Turkish Armenia.
    Signed by Lenin, Stalin, Bonch-Bruevich and Gorbunov in P*, Dec. 31, 1917; hence not specifically attributable to Stalin.

252. O "Turetskoi Armenii. " ["Turkish Armenia. "]
    Article signed "I. Dzhugashvili-Stalin" in P*, Dec. 31, 1917.

1918

253. Statement in Central Committee, Jan. 11, 1918.
    See appendix "A, " containing full list of Stalin's recorded published statements in the Central Committee.
    IV, 27.

254. O kievskoi burzhuaznoi rade. [The Kiev Bourgeois Rada.]
    Signed article in P*, Jan. 13, 1918.
    IV, 28-29.

255. Statements at Third All-Russian Congress of Soviets, Jan. 10-18, 1918.

    Report on the national question, Jan. 15. P. 31, line 31, should read: "...na neobkhodimost' ogranicheniia printsipa samoopredeleniia..."
    IV, 30-32.

Draft Resolution on the Russian Federation, Jan. 15.
IV, 32-33.

Conclusion, Jan. 15.
IV, 33-37.

Above are in P*, Jan. 17, 18, 1918.

256. Correction on letter from Lenin to Trotsky, Jan. 28, 1918.
LS*, XI, 25.

257*. Telegram to Nizhneudinsk Soviet, Feb. 14, 1918.
Signed by Lenin and Stalin, published in LS*, XXXIV, 16, which states that original was in Stalin's hand.

258. Teletype conversation with members of Dvisnk Soviet, Feb. 18, 1918.
Statements by Lenin and Stalin given collectively in version in LS*, XXXIV, 17-18 (that is, the two names are put down together as if they constituted one conversationalist).

259. Telephone message to Petrograd Committee of Party, Feb. 21, 1918.
Signed Lenin, Stalin.
IV, 38 (published for first time).

260. Telegram to secretariat of Ukrainian Soviet Republic, Feb. 21, 1918.
Signed, published in Dokumenty o razgrome germanskikh okkupantov na Ukraine v 1918 g. (Moscow, Gospolitizdat, 1942).
IV, 39-40.

261. Teletype message to secretariat of Ukrainian Soviet Republic, Feb. 24, 1918.
Signed, partly published in Stalin, Stat'i i rechi ob Ukraine. Sbornik (Kiev. Izd. Ts. K. KP(b)U 1936), p. 231, which

*Starting with this entry all dates are New Style.

cites <u>Vestnik Ukrainskoi Narodnoi Respubliki</u>, Feb. 26, 1918.
First published in full in <u>S</u>.
IV, 41-44.

262.   Telegram to Rostov-na-Donu, Feb. 28, 1918.
Signed by Lenin and Stalin, published in Lenin, <u>Sochineniia</u>
3rd ed. but not the fourth. Third ed. states that it <u>was first</u>
published in V.A. Antonov-Ovseenko, <u>Zapiski o grazhdanskoi</u>
<u>voine</u>, vol. III (no further information).

263.   Ob otkrytii Vserossiiskogo S''ezda Sovetov. [The Opening of
the All-Russian Congress of Soviets.]
In <u>Vestnik Ukrainskoi Narodnoi Respubliki</u>, March 3,
1917, according to <u>Proletarskaia Revoliutsiia</u>, p. 182.

264.   Ukrainskii uzel. [The Ukrainian Knot.]
Signed article in <u>I</u>*, March 14, 1917.
IV, 45-48.

265.   Finliandskaia revoliutsiia i nash sotsial-kornilovtsy'. [The
Finnish Revolution and Our Social-Kornilovites.]
Article in <u>Petrogradskaia Pravda</u>, no. 50, 1918, according to <u>Kniga i Proletarskaia Revoliutsiia</u>, no. 12, 1939,
p. 135. No information on signature.

266.   Letter to Petrovskii, Spring, 1918.
Signed letter to Commissar of Internal Affairs in Tsarytsin
published in I. Martynov, <u>Respublika v povolzh'e</u>* (Stalingrad, 1933), p. 22.

267.   O Tataro-bashkirskoi Sovetskoi Respublike. [A Tatar-Bashkir
Soviet Republic.]
Signed article in <u>P</u>*, March 23, 1918. Following last line,
p. 50, the following should appear: "Publikuia nizhesleduiush-
chee 'Polozhenie', schitaiu nuzhnym soobshchit', chto analo-
gichnye 'Polozheniia' vyrabotyvaiutsia Narodnym Komissari-
atom po delam Natsional'nostei dlia azerbaidzhanskikh tatar,
gruzin, armian, kirgiz, sarto-tekintsev i drugikh narodov
Rossii, revoliutsionnye organizatsii kotorykh proshu svoi
konkretnye plany federatsii. "
IV, 49-50.

268. Polozhenie o Tataro-Bashkirskoi Sovetskoi Respubliki Rossiiskoi Sovetskoi Federatsii. [Statute on the Tatar-Bashkir Soviet
Republic of the Russian Soviet Federation.]
  Signed by Stalin, Mulla-Nur-Bakhitov, Manatov, Ibragi-
mov and Dimanshtein, published in P*, March 23, 1917. Not
a personal statement, but closely related to Stalin's statements in the previous entry.

269. Note to Lenin, March 23, 1918.
  LS*, XXXV, 17

270. Kontrrevoliutsionery Zakavkaz'ia pod maskoi sotsializma.
[Caucasian Counterrevolutionaries under a Socialist Mask.]
  Signed article in P*, March 26, 27, 1918.
IV, 51-65.

271. Teletype Conversation with Iur'ev, April, 1918.
  Published in K.E. Voroshilov, Stalin i Krasnaia Armiia*
(Moscow, Voenizdat, 2nd ed., 1937), pp. 165-166.

272. Ob ocherednoi zadache Sovetskoi Vlastii. [The Next Task of
the Soviet Regime.]
  An article or message addressed to the Soviets of Kazan,
Orenburg, Ekaterinburg and the Sovnarkom of the Turkestan
krai "and to others," signed and dated "April, 1918." Published in Politika Sovetskoi Vlasti po natsional'nomu voprosu
za tri goda* (Moscow, 1920), pp. 8-9. In connection with the
non-appearance of this item in S it may be noted that the
article was reprinted in the journal Revoliutsiia i Natsional'
nosti, no. 11, 1937, pp. 116-117. This number is missing
from sets of this journal in America, and the Hoover
Institution Library was informed by Amkniga, an official
agency, that the number was not issued for "technical
reasons." Actually, it was published and was seen by the
present writer in the Lenin Library. One is free to wonder
whether or not the presence of this particular article by
Stalin has any connection with the export embargo on this
issue of Revoliutsiia i Natsional'nosti.

273. Na Kavkaze. [In the Caucasus.]
  Statement to Izvestiia correspondent, definitely attributed
to Stalin, published in I*, April 2, 1918.

274. Telegram to Ekaterinburg and Krasnoiarsk Soviet Deputies, April 2, 1918.
     Signed by Lenin and Stalin in LS*, XXXV, 18.

275. Telegram to Ekaterinburg and Krasnoiarsk Soviet Deputies, April 3, 1918.
     Signed by Lenin and Stalin in LS*, XXXV, 18.

276. Organizatsiia Rossiiskoi Federativnoi Respubliki. [Organizatio of a Russian Federal Republic.]
     Interview in P*, April 3, 4, 1918.
     IV, 66-73.

277. Statement in Trial of Martov for Slander.
     Verbatim quotation of Stalin's statement appears in account of trial in P*, April 5, 1918.

278. Statement in Trial of Martov for Slander.
     Indirect but clear quotations of Stalin's statement appears in account of trial in P*, April 6, 1918.

279. Telegram on Ukraine, April 6, 1918.
     Signed, published in Istoriia KP(b)U* (Kiev, Institut istorii partii, 1933), vol. II, pp. 459-460.

280. Telegram to Vernyi Soviet deputies, April 7, 1918.
     Published in Zaria Svobody (Vernyi), April 14, 1918, according to Kniga i Proletarskaia Revoliutsiia, p. 135.

281. Odna iz ocherednykh zadach. [One Immediate Task.]
     Signed article in P*, April 9, 1918.
     IV, 74-78.

282. Decree establishing "Chrezvychainyi komissariat iuzhnogo raiona" (and appointing Ordzonikidze commissar).
     In P*, April 12, 1918, signed by Lenin and Stalin.

283. O tipe Rossiiskoi Sovetskoi Respubliki. [The Character of the
Russian Soviet Republic.]
Theses of April 12, 1918, submitted to committee on
RSFSR constitution, published in G.S. Gurvich, Istoriia
Sovetskoi Konstitutsii* (Moscow, 1923), pp. 146-147.

284. Decree no. 325 of Commissar of Nationality Affairs.
Published in Bor'ba (Tsaritsyn), April 14, 1918, according to Proletarskaia Revoliutsiia, p. 182. Signed "Narodnyi
Komissar po Delam Natsional'nostei" rather than "Stalin, "
so may not be directly attributable to him.

285. Obshchie polozheniia konstitutsii Rossiiskoi Sovetskoi Federativnoi Respubliki. [General Provisions of the Constitution of
the Russian Soviet Federative Republic.]
Submitted in mid-April to committee on new constitution,
published in G.S. Gurvich, Istoriia Sovetskoi Konstitutsii
(Moscow, 1923), pp. 147-148. This entry is an earlier draft
of the document noted in the following entry.

286. Obshchie polozheniia konstitutsii Rossiiskoi Sotsialisticheskoi
Federativnoi Sovetskoi Respubliki. [General Provisions of the
Constitution of the Russian Socialist Federative Soviet Republic.]
Unsigned statement in I*, April 25, 1918. Previous entry
is Stalin's earlier draft, and is presumably closer to his
own thought since a commission participated in the revisions.
According to IV, 418, fn. 14, the revised resolution was
adopted on April 19.
IV, 79-80.

287. Telegram to the Fifth Congress of Soviets of the Turkestan Krai,
April 22, 1918.
Signed by Lenin and Stalin, in I*, April 26, 1918.
IV, 81.

288. Decree ending the Milli Shuro.
P*, April 26, 1918.

289. Interview with Volga-German Colonists.
Indirect but clear quotations from Stalin's answers to
colonists in P*, April 30, 1918.

290.   Telegram from Russian Peace Delegation to Ukraine.
          Signed by Stalin, Rakovskii, Manuilskii, in P*, May 1,
       1918.

291.   Decree establishing Moslem Worker-Peasant Army, May 2,
       1918.
          Signed, in Bor'ba Klassov*, no. 11, 1934, p. 96.

292.   Kto vinovat v ottiazhke mirnykh peregovorov s Ukrainoi? [Who
       Is to Blame for the Delay in the Peace Negotiations with the
       Ukraine?]
          Interview in Bednota*, May 4, 1918.

293.   Telegram to Antonov's Adjutant, May 5, 1918.
          Signed by Lenin and Stalin, in LS*, XVIII, 67-68.

294.   Draft of Radiogram to Peace Delegation at Kursk, May 6, 1918.
          Rough sketch in LS*, XI, 74.

295.   Telegram to Secretary of Peace Delegation, May 8, 1918.
          Signed by Lenin and Stalin, in LS*, XXXIV, 23.

296.   Mirnye peregovory s Ukrainoi. [Peace Negotiations with the
       Ukraine.]
          Interview in I*, May 9, 1918.
       IV, 82-84.

297.   Statements at Constituent Congress of Tatar-Bashkir Soviet
       Republic, May 10-16, 1918.

          Speech at opening of congress, May 10. In P*, May 18,
          1918. P. 86, line 9: "drugikh" should read "otstal'nykh."
       IV, 85-90.

          Speech at close of congress, May 16. In P*, May 24, 1918
       IV, 90-92.

298.   Ocherednaia lozh'. [Another Lie.]
          Signed article in P*, May 19, 1918.
       IV, 93-94.

299.   Polozhenie na Kavkaze. [The Situation in the Caucasus.]
             Signed article in P*, May 23, 1918; p. 98, line 14:
        "russkie" should read "bashkiry"; p. 99, line 8: "(ne
        shutite!)" interpolated in S.
        IV, 95-100.

300.   K polozheniiu na Kavkaze. [Concerning the Situation in the
        Caucasus.]
             Signed article in P*, May 28, 1918.
        IV, 101-103.

301.   Telephone Message to Tsaritsyn, May 29, 1918.
             Signed message in Dokumenty po istorii grazhdanskoi
        voiny v SSSR* (Moscow, Gos. izd. pol. lit., 1940), vol. I,
        p. 154.

302.   O donshchine i Severnom Kavkaze'. [The Don and the North
        Caucasus.]
             Signed article in P*, June 1, 1918. Order of paragraphs,
        pp. 112-115, has been changed, but meaning is essentially
        as in S.

303.   Telegram to Tsaritsyn, June 3, 1918.
             Signed published in Dokumenty...Tsaritsyna*, p. 44.

304.   Telegram to Lenin, June 4, 1918.
             Signed, published in Proletarskaia Revoliutsiia*, no. 7,
        1936, p. 73.

305.   Telegram to Lenin, June 5, 1918.
             Signed, published in Dokumenty...Tsaritsyna*, p. 44.

306.   Telegram to Lenin, June 6, 1918.
             Signed, published in Proletarskaia Revoliutsiia*, no. 7,
        1936, p. 74.

307.   Telegram to Lenin, June 7, 1918.
             Signed, published in Proletarskaia Revoliutsiia*, no. 7,
        1936, p. 75.
        IV, 116-117.

308.   Telegram to Lenin, June 7, 1918.
            Signed, published in <u>Dokumenty</u>...<u>Tsaritsyna</u>*, p. 46.
        Corrects statement at close of preceding telegram.

309.   Telegram to Lenin, June 9, 1918.
            Signed, published in <u>Dokumenty po istorii grazhdanskoi
        voiny</u>* (Moscow, Gos. izd. pol. lit., 1940), I, 156-157.

310.   An Inquiry on the Situation in Turkestan and Transcaucasia.
            Presumably a message, published in <u>Bakinsii Rabochii</u>,
        June 9, 1918, according to <u>Proletarskaia Revoliutsiia</u>, p.
        183.

311.   Telegram to Lenin and Tsiurupa, June 10, 1918.
            Signed, published in <u>Dokumenty</u>...<u>Tsaritsyna</u>*, p.49.

312.   Telegram to Shaumian, June 10, 1918.
            Published in <u>Bakinskii Rabochii</u>, June 11, 1918, accord-
        ing <u>Proletarskaia Revoliutsiia</u>, p. 183. Republished in
        <u>Istorik Marksist</u>*, no. 5, 1938, p. 46. Positive identificatior
        of author in text of message.

313.   Telegram to Lenin, June 13, 1918.
            Signed, published in <u>Dokumenty</u>...<u>Tsaritsyna</u>*, pp. 51-52

314.   Telegram to Lenin, June 15, 1918.
            Signed by Stalin and Ordzhonikidze, "3 am of the night of
        June 14-15," published in <u>Dokumenty</u>...<u>Tsaritsyna</u>*, p. 53.

315.   Telegram to Lenin, June 15, 1918.
            Signed, published in <u>Dokumenty</u>...<u>Tsaritsyna</u>*, pp. 52-53

316.   Telegram to Lenin, June 15, 1918.
            Signed, published in <u>Dokumenty</u>...<u>Tsaritsyna</u>*, p. 53.
        (Not a duplicate of preceding entry.)

317.   Convocation of Conference of Representatives of Soviets of Don
        Region, June 17, 1918.
            Signed by Stalin and Ordzhonikidze, published in Bor'ba,
        June 18, 1918; republished in Dokumenty...Tsaritsyna*,
        p. 59.

318.   Telegram to Lenin and Tsiurupa, June 17, 1918.
            Signed by Stalin and Iakubov, published in Dokumenty...
        Tsaritsyna*, p. 58.

319.   Telegram to Tsiurupa, June 18, 1918.
            Signed, published in Dokumenty...Tsaritsyna*, p. 59.

320.   Telegram to Lenin and Tsiurupa, June 19, 1918.
            Signed, published in Dokumenty...Tsaritsyna, * p. 65.

321.   Telegram to Lenin, June 21, 1918.
            Signed by Stalin and Iakubov, published in Dokumenty...
        Tsaritsyna*, p. 69.

322.   Decree of June 22, 1918.
            Signed by Stalin and Alliluev, published in Bor'ba
        (Tsaritsyn), June 26, 1918, and Dokumenty...Tsaritsyna*,
        pp. 68-69.

323.   Telegram to Lenin, June 22, 1918.
            Signed, published in Dokumenty...Tsaritsyna*, pp. 70-71.

324.   Confirmation of Military Order, June 23, 1918.
            Signed, published in Melikov*, p. 70.

325.   Telegram to Tsiurupa, June 24, 1918.
            Signed, published in Dokumenty...Tsaritsyna*, p. 71.

326.   Telegram to Tsiurupa, June 26, 1918.
            Signed, published in Dokumenty...Tsaritsyna*, p. 71.

327.   Telegram to Tsiurupa, June 26, 1918.
          Signed, Dokumenty...Tsaritsyna*, pp. 71-72.

328.   Telegram to Lenin, June 29, 1918.
          Signed, published in Dokumenty...Tsaritsyna*, p. 72.

329.   Message to Chicherin, June 30, 1918.
          Signed, published in Dokumenty...Tsaritsyna*, p. 76.
       Presumably telegram or teletype.

330.   Teletype Message to Chicherin, July 1, 1918.
          Signed, published in S.G. Shaumian, Bakinskaia kommuna
       (Baku, Krasnyi Vostok, 1927), p. 38.

331.   Message to the Defense Staff (presumably in Tsaritsyn), July 1,
       1918.
          Signed, published in Dokumenty...Tsaritsyna*, p. 78.

332.   Message to Moscow, July 4, 1918.
          Signed, published in Dokumenty...Tsaritsyna*, p. 80.
       Presumably by telegram or teletype.

333.   Letter to Lenin, July 7, 1918.
          Signed, partially published in P* Dec. 21, 1929, and fully
       in Dokumenty...Tsaritsyna*, pp. 80-81, which confirm
       essentially the same message as in S.
       IV, 118-119.

334.   Letter to Shaumian, July 8, 1918.
          Signed, published in Dokumenty...Tsaritsyna*, pp. 80-81

335.   Certification of Voroshilov as Commander of Front, July 10,
       1918.
          Signed with facsimile copy in Dokumenty...Tsaritsyna*,
          p. 82.

336.   Letter to Lenin, July 10, 1918.
          Signed, first published in S.
       IV, 120-121.

337.   Telegram to Lenin, July 11, 1918.
        Excerpts published in Dokumenty...Tsaritsyna*, p. 84.

338.   Message to Lenin, July 15, 1918.
        Excerpt quoted in N. Vokov, "Iz istorii Krasnogo voz-
        dushnogo flota, " Propagandist i Agitator RKKA*, no. 14,
        1939, p. 12.

339.   Telegram to Lenin, July 16, 1918.
        Signed, published in Dokumenty...Tsaritsyna*, p. 84.

340.   Message to Shaumian, July 20, 1918.
        Signed, published in Bakinskii Rabochii, July 22, 1918,
        according to Proletarskaia Revoliutsiia, p. 184. Republished
        in E. Burdzhalov, Dvadtsat' shest' bakinskikh komissarov*
        (Moscow, Gos. izd. pol. lit., 1938), p. 79.

341.   Telegram to Lenin, July 21, 1918.
        Signed, published in Dokumenty...Tsaritsyna*, p. 85.
        Includes text of telegram to Shaumian, July 20, and covering
        message.

342.   Teletype Reply to Question from Lenin, July 24, 1918.
        Signed, published in LS*, XVIII, 193.

343.   Telegram to Lenin, July 26, 1918.
        Signed, excerpts of various portions of this document ap-
        pear in Melikov*, pp. 119-120, and Dokumenty...Tsaritsyna, *
        p. 91.

344.   Telegram to Lenin, July 28.
        Signed, published in Dokumenty...Tsaritsyna*, p. 94.

345.   Statement to Delegation from Soviet Government of the Don,
        July 30, 1918.
        Signed, published in Dokumenty...Tsaritsyna*, p. 96.

346.   Telegram (presumably to Moscow), July 31, 1918.
       Signed, published in Dokumenty...Tsaritsyna*, p. 97.

347.   Letter to Lenin, Aug. 4, 1918.
       First published in LS*, XVIII, 197.
       IV, 122-126.

348.   Order of North Caucasus Military District, Aug. 5.
       Signed, published in Bor'ba (Tsaritsyn), according to
       Proletarskaia Revoliutsiia, p. 184; republished in Dokument
       ...Tsaritsyna*, p. 103.

349.   Letter to Lenin, Aug. 7, 1918.
       Signed, published in Dokumenty...Tsaritsyna*, p. 107.

350.   Mandate for Parkhomenko, Aug. 7, 1918.
       Signed, published in Dokumenty...Tsaritsyna*, p. 107.

351.   Note to Marochkin, Aug. 10, 1918.
       Signed, published in Dokumenty...Tsaritsyna*, p. 111.

352.   Order to Tsaritsyn Commissars and Commanders, Aug. 11,
       1918.
       Signed by Stalin and Voroshilov, published in Dokumenty..
       Tsaritsyna*, p. 112. Confusingly, Melikov*, pp. 143-145,
       quotes at length from a document supposedly signed by Stalin
       and Voroshilov and, in part, written in "the clear, Stalin
       style, " which is different in content, while bearing the same
       date and order number (14).

353.   Order to North Caucasus Military District, Aug. 11.
       Signed by Stalin and Voroshilov, published in Dokumenty..
       Tsaritsyna*, p. 112.

354.   Teletype Conversation with Vasiliev, Aug. 11, 1918.
       Positive identification in published version, Dokumenty...
       Tsaritsyna*, p. 113.

355. Teletype Conversation with Unidentified Official, Aug. 12, 1918.
Positive identification of Stalin in published version,
Dokumenty...Tsaritsyna*, pp. 114-115.

356. Order of North Caucasus Military Soviet, Aug. 13.
Signed by Stalin and Voroshilov, published in Dokumenty
...Tsaritsyna*, p. 115.

357. Order of North Caucasus Military Soviet, Aug. 14, 1918.
Signed, published in Dokumenty...Tsaritsyna*, p. 117.

358. Bulletin of the Military Soviet of the North Caucasus District,
Aug. 15, 1918.
Signed by Stalin and Voroshilov, first published in Soldat
Revoliutsii (Tsaritsyn), Aug. 15, 1918, according to
Proletarskaia Revoliutsiia, p. 184; republished in Dokumenty
...Tsaritsyna*, p. 118.

359. Order to North Caucasus Military District, Aug. 16, 1918.
According to Melikov*, p. 195, Stalin and Voroshilov
issued an order of this date, from which a substantial excerpt is quoted. However, no signature is given, and it is
not clear how directly this order, which is a fairly technical
military one, is attributable to Stalin.

360. Order to Kharchenko, Aug. 16, 1918.
Signed, published in Dokumenty...Tsaritsyna*, p. 122.

361. Order to Mezhevykh, Aug. 17, 1918.
Signed by Stalin and Voroshilov, published in Dokumenty
...Tsaritsyna*, p. 124.

362. Order to Echelon Commanders of Kolpakov's brigade, Aug. 17,
1918.
Signed by Stalin and Voroshilov, published in Dokumenty...
Tsaritsyna*, p. 124.

363. Order of Aug. 18, 1918.
     Signed by Stalin and Voroshilov, published in Dokumenty
     ...Tsaritsyna*, p. 127.

364. Decree of Military Soviet, Aug. 22, 1918.
     Signed by Stalin and Voroshilov, published in Dokumenty
     ...Tsaritsyna*, p. 134.

365. Order of Military Soviet of North Caucasus Military District,
     Aug. 23, 1918.
     Signed by Stalin and Voroshilov, published in Dokumenty
     ...Tsaritsyna*, p. 135.

366. Order to Commander of Central District, Aug. 24, 1918.
     Signed by Stalin and Voroshilov, according to Melikov*,
     p. 155, which quotes what appears to be the entire order.

367. Telegram to Parkhomenko, Aug. 26, 1918.
     Signed, published in Dokumenty...Tsaritsyna*, p. 138.

368. Message to Kharchenko and Kolpakov, Aug. 29, 1918.
     According to Proletarskaia Revoliutsiia, p. 184,
     Prozhektor, no. 3-4, 1933, p. 12, contains this document,
     signed by Stalin and Voroshilov.

369. Order of Military Soviet of North Caucasus Military District,
     Aug. 30, 1931.
     According to Melikov*, pp. 156-157, Stalin and Voroshilo
     issued this order, which appears to be published in full, but
     without signatures. It is not clear to what extent this rather
     technical military document is attributable to Stalin.

370. Directive to Air Command, Aug. 30, 1918.
     Signed, published in Dokumenty...Tsaritsyna*, p. 141.

371. Order of Military Soviet of North Caucasian Military District,
     Aug. 30, 1918.
     Signed by Stalin and Voroshilov, first published in Soldat

Revoliutsii (Tsaritsyn), Aug. 30, 1918, according to Proletarskaia Revoliutsiia, p. 185; republished in Dokumenty...Tsaritsyna*, pp. 140-141.

372. Letter to Lenin, Aug. 31, 1918.
      Signed, first published in B*, no. 2, 1938.
      IV, 127.

373. Telegram to Sverdlov, Aug. 31, 1918.
      Signed, first published in Soldat Revoliutsii (Tsaritsyn),
      Sept. 1, 1918, according to S.
      IV, 128.

374. Order to Chief of Staff of Volga Fleet, Sept. 2, 1918.
      Issue by Stalin and Voroshilov, according to Melikov*,
      p. 158, which publishes document without signature. Unclear
      to what extent it is attributable to Stalin.

375. Telegram to the Sovnarkom, Sept. 6, 1918.
      Signed, first published in Proletarskaia Revoliutsiia*,
      no. 1, 1939, p. 101, which dates the message Sept. 7.
      IV 129.

376. Order of Military Soviet of North Caucasus Military District,
      Sept. 6, 1918.
      Signed by Stalin and Voroshilov, first published in Bor'ba
      (Tsaritsyn), Sept. 18, 1918, according to Proletarskaia
      Revoliutsiia, p. 185. Republished in Dokumenty...Tsaritsyna,
      pp. 149-150.

377. Telegram to Lenin, Sept. 7, 1918.
      Signed, published in Dokumenty...Tsaritsyna*, 151.

378. Order to Kharchenko, Sept. 7, 1918.
      Signed by Stalin and Voroshilov, according to Melikov*,
      p. 163, which includes document without signatures. It is a
      technical military command that was given to Kharchenko to
      issue in his own name, and Stalin's connection is dubious.

379.   Telegram to Lenin and Sverdlov, Sept. 8, 1918.
        Evidently from Stalin and Voroshilov in name of Military
    Soviet of North Caucasus Military District, but not signed
    by any individual, judging by Melikov*, p. 162 and Doku-
    menty...Tsaritsyna*, p. 151. According to Melikov, first
    published in Soldat Revoliutsii (Tsaritsyn), Sept. 10, 1918.

380.   Order of Military Soviet of North Caucasus Military District,
    Sept. 8, 1918.
        Signed by Stalin and Voroshilov, published in Dokumenty.
    Tsaritsyna*, p. 151.

381.   Order of Military Soviet of North Caucasus Military District,
    Sept. 10, 1918.
        Signed by Stalin and Voroshilov, published in Dokumenty.
    Tsaritsyna*, pp. 153-154.

382.   Order of Military Soviet of North Caucasus Military District,
    Sept. 10, 1918.
        Signed by Stalin and Voroshilov, published in Soldat Revo
    liutsii (Tsaritsyn), Sept. 13, 1918, according to Proletarsk
    Revoliutsiia, p. 185.

383.   Teletype Conversation with Voroshilov, Sept. 15, 1918.
        Positive identification of Stalin in published version,
    Dokumenty...Tsaritsyna*, pp. 160-161.

384.   Telegram to Voroshilov, Sept. 15, 1918.
        Signed, published in Dokumenty...Tsaritsyna*, p. 161.

385.   Telegram to Voroshilov, Sept. 19, 1918.
        Signed by Lenin and Stalin, first published in I*, Sept. 21
    1918.
    IV, 130.

386.   Na iuzhnom fronte. [The Southern Front.]
        Interview in I*, Sept. 21, 1918.
    IV, 131-133.

387.   Resolution of Revolutionary Military Council of the Southern
Front, ca. Sept. 22-24, 1918.
        Signed by Stalin and Voroshilov, published in <u>Dokumenty</u>
...Tsaritsyna*, p. 164.

388.   Order of the Military-Revolutionary Soviet of the Southern
Front, Sept. 27, 1918.
        Signed by Stalin and Voroshilov, published in Melikov*,
p. 187.

389.   Message to the Military-Revolutionary Soviet of the Republic
(Moscow), Sept. 27, 1918.
        Signed by Stalin and Voroshilov, published in <u>Dokumenty</u>
...Tsaritsyna*, p. 167. Also signed by S. Minin, according
to version in <u>Voina i Revoliutsiia</u>, May-June, 1935, p. 5.

390.   Order of the Military-Revolutionary Soviet of the Southern
Front, Oct. 1, 1918.
        Contained, with signatures of Stalin and Voroshilov, in
teletype conversation between Voroshilov and Kharchenko,
published in <u>P</u>*, Jan. 3, 1935.

391.   Telegram to Military-Revolutionary Soviet of the Republic
(Moscow), Oct. 2, 1918.
        Signed by Stalin and Voroshilov, published in <u>Dokumenty</u>...
<u>Tsaritsyna</u>*, pp. 169-170.

392.   Telegram to Lenin, Sverdlov, Central Committee, Arzamas,
Military-Revolutionary Soviet of the Republic, Oct. 3, 1918.
        Signed by Stalin and Voroshilov, published in Melikov*,
p. 197. Partly a covering letter for order from Trotsky and
reply of Military Soviet of Southern Front. The highly political content would imply that Stalin was the principal author.

393.   Telegram to Lenin, Oct. 3, 1917.
        Signed by Stalin and Voroshilov, published in <u>Dokumenty</u>...
<u>Tsaritsyna</u>*, pp. 170-171. The highly political content would
imply that Stalin was the principal author.

394.   Telegram to Arzamas, Oct. 4, 1918.
          Signed, published in Melikov*, p. 200.

395.   Order of Military-Revolutionary Soviet of Southern Front,
          Oct. 5, 1918.
              Signed by Stalin and Voroshilov, published in Dokumenty...
          Tsaritsyna*, p. 171

396.   Telegram to Voroshilov, Oct. 6, 1918.
              Signed, published in Dokumenty...Tsaritsyna*, p. 172.

397.   Message to Tsaritsyn, Oct. 8, 1918.
              Signed, first published in Soldat Revoliutsii, Oct. 9, 1918,
          according to Proletarskaia Revoliutsiia, p. 186. Republished
          in Dokumenty...Tsaritsyna*, p. 172.

398.   Teletype Conversation with Sverdlov, Oct. 11, 1918.
              Positive identification in version published in Dokumenty...
          Tsaritsyna*, pp. 172-173.

399.   Telegram to Lenin and Sverdlov, Oct. 12, 1918.
              Signed, published in Dokumenty...Tsaritsyna*, p. 173.

400.   Order to Troops on Tsaritsyn front, Oct. 15, 1918.
              Signed, first published in Bor'ba (Tsaritsyn), Oct. 17,
          1918, according to Melikov*, pp. 222-223, where it is re-
          published.

401.   Telegram to Lenin, Sverdlov, the Military-Revolutionary Soviet,
          Oct. 15, 1918.
              Signed by Stalin, Voroshilov and Minin, according to
          Voina i Revoliutsiia*, May-June, 1935, pp. 4-5, which re-
          produces the document in full.

402.   Pis'mo k donskoi bednote. [Letter to the Poor of the Don Region.
              Proclamatory letter in Soldat Revoliutsii (Tsaritsyn),
          Oct. 16, 1918, signed by Stalin and Voroshilov, according to
          Dokumenty...Tsaritsyna*, pp. 178-179, in which it is re-
          published.

403.   Telegram to Lenin and Sverdlov, Oct. 18, 1918.
            Signed, published in Dokumenty...Tsaritsyna*, p. 179.

404.   Telegram to Lenin or Sovnarkom, Oct. 19, 1918.
            Signed, published in Dokumenty...Tsaritsyna*, p. 176.

405.   Order to Kolpakov, Oct. 19, 1918.
            Signed, published in Melikov*, p. 232.

406.   Message (presumably telegram) to Voroshilov, Oct. 22, 1918.
            Signed, published in Dokumenty...Tsaritsyna*, p. 184.

407.   Letter to Karl Liebknecht, Oct. 23, 1918.
            Signed by Lenin, Stalin and Sverdlov, published in Lenin,
        Sochineniia*, 3rd ed., XXIX, p. 515, which implies that it
        was chiefly his work.

408.   Order of the Military-Revolutionary Soviet of the Southern
        Front, Oct. 24, 1918.
            Signed by Stalin and Voroshilov, published in I*, Jan. 3,
        1935. Date implies that Stalin's signature was a formality
        since he had left the front for Moscow five days before.

409.   Logika veshchei. [The Logic of Facts.]
            Signed article in P*, Oct. 29, 1918.
        IV, 134-145.

410.   Speech to Moscow Soviet, Oct. 29, 1918.
            I*, Oct. 30, 1918.
        IV, 146-147.

411.   O iuge Rossii. [The South of Russia.]
            P*, Oct. 30, in which it is headlined "Stalin o iuge Rossii."
        IV, 148-151.

412.   Letter to Spartakists, late Oct., 1918.
            Signed by Lenin, Trotsky, Stalin, Bukharin, and Sverdlov,

published in <u>Bor'ba Bol'shevikov za sozdanie kommunisti-</u>
<u>cheskogo internatsionala 1914-1919*</u> (Moscow, 1934), pp.
103-104. Unlikely to have been Stalin's work in any direct
sense.

413.   Teletype Conversation with Voroshilov, early November, 1918.
        Positive identification in version published in Melikov*,
        pp. 265-266.

414.   Speech to Congress of Moslem Communists, Nov. 5, 1918.
        Positive identification in first published version, <u>ZN</u>*,
        Nov. 24, 1918.

415.   Teletype Conversation with Voroshilov, Nov. 6, 1918.
        Positive identification in excerpt published in <u>Dokumenty</u>
        ...<u>Tsaritsyna</u>*, p. 189.

416.   Oktiabr'skii perevorot. [The October Revolution.]
        Signed article in <u>P</u>*, Nov. 6, 1918. P. 154: Stalin became
        confused on precise dates in the original and had the sur-
        render of the Winter Palace occurring early on Oct. 25
        rather than Oct. 26 (OS). Correction of this error required
        not only revision of the dates but also the transposition of
        two paragraphs. Also, p. 154, the following should appear
        following line 20: "Vsia rabota po prakticheskoi organizatsii
        vostaniia prokhodila pod neposredstvennym rukovodstvom
        predsedatelia Petrogradsk. Soveta t. Trotskogo. Mozhno s
        uvernost'iu skazat', chto bystrym perekhodom garnizona na
        storonu Soveta i umeloi postanovkoi raboty Voenno-Revo-
        liutsionnogo Komiteta partiia obiazana prezhde vsego i
        glavnym obrazom tov. Trotskomu. Tovarishchi Antonov i
        Podvoiskii byli glavnymi pomoshchnikami tovarishcha
        Trotskogo. "
        IV, 152-154.

417.   Oktiabr'skii perevorot i natsional'nyi vopros. [The October
        Revolution and the National Question.]
        An article bearing this title appears in <u>S</u>, IV, 155-167;
        it is, however, a composite of two signed articles that were
        published in <u>P</u> , in Nov., 1917:
            (a) Oktiabr'skii perevorot i natsional'nyi vopros--
        Nov. 6, 1918.

(b) Oktiabr'skii perevorot i vopros o natsional'nostiakh
--Nov. 19, 1918.

The second of these duplicates some passages from the
first, but omits some and adds others. The composite version in S is drawn mainly from the second, although the
opening paragraph is from the first. The effect is to omit
significant portions of the first article from S, while using
its title--without informing the reader that this is the case.
Rather than attempt a cumbersome listing of the passages
that were omitted in this process, the present bibliographer
has provided a full text of the article of Nov. 6 in appendix
"B." It should be added that the composite article appearing
in S was not concocted by the editors of S, but appeared as
early as the publication of the anthology Marksizm i natsional'no-kolonial'nyi vopros (Moscow, Partizdat, 1935).

418.   Sredostenie. [Partition Wall.]
            Signed article in ZN*, Nov. 17, 1918.
        IV, 168-170.

419.   Oktiabr'skii perevorot i vopros o natsional'nostiakh. [The
        October Revolution and the Question of the Nationalities.]
            See No. 417.

420.   Ne zabyvaite vostoka. [Don't Forget the East.]
            Unsigned article in ZN*, Nov. 24, 1918.
        IV, 171-173.

421.   Teletype Message to Zatonskii, Nov. 28, 1918.
            Letopis' Revoliutsii*, no. 1 (10), 1925, p. 148.

422.   Ukraina osvobozhdaetsia. [The Ukraine Is Liberating Itself.]
            Signed article in ZN*, Dec. 1, 1918.
        IV, 174-176.

423.   Osvobozhdaetsia Ukraina. [The Ukraine Liberating Itself.]
            Signed, published in P*, Dec. 1, 1918; generally the
        same substance as "Osvobozhdaetsia Ukraina, " appearing
        in Zhizn' Natsional'nostei on the same date, but considerably
        revised in style.

424.   Decree of the Cartridge Commission of the Soviet of Defense,
        Dec. 5, 1918.
                Signed by Lenin, Stalin and Krasin, published in LS*,
        XXXIV, 55-57. A formal signature as commission member.

425.   Telegram to the Samara Gubernia Military Committee, Dec. 7,
        1918.
                Signed by Lenin and Stalin, published in LS*, XXXIV, 59.

426.   Decree of Soviet of Defense, Dec. 11, 1918.
                Signed by Lenin and Stalin, published in LS*, XXXIV,
        62. A formal signature as member of the Soviet.

427.   Instruction issued by Commissariat of Nationality Affairs,
        Dec. 15, 1918.
                Signed by Stalin and Tovtsukha, published in ZN*,
        Dec. 15, 1918.

428.   S vostoka svet. [Light from the East.]
                Signed article in ZN*, Dec. 15, 1918. P. 179, last para.
        p. 180, lines 1-3, 15-20; p. 181, lines 10-15, 21-32, have
        all been added in S (i.e., these lines did not occur in origi-
        nal version).
        IV, 177-182.

429.   Teletype Message to Dvinsk, Dec. 18, 1918.
                Signed by Lenin and Stalin, published in LS*, XXXIV, 59.

430.   Decree of Soviet of Defense, Dec. 19, 1918.
                Signed by Lenin and Stalin, published in I*, Dec. 19,
        1918. A memorandum by Lenin in LS, XXXIV, 69, makes
        it clear that this decree was basically a report by Stalin to
        the Soviet.

431.   Dela idut. [Things Are Moving.]
                Unsigned article in ZN*, Dec. 22, 1918.
        IV, 183-185.

432.   Interview with Estonian Delegation.
          ZN*, Dec. 29, 1918, contains what appears to be an
        abridged account of what Stalin told the Estonians.

                        1919

433.   Telegram to Lenin, "early Jan., 1919."
          Signed by Stalin and Dzerzhinskii, published in K 25-
        letiiu osvobozhdeniia udmurtii iz kolchakovshchiny (Izhevsk,
        1939), p. 17, according to Proletarskaia Revoliutsiia, p.
        187, which heads the citation: "Iz Glazova. Moskva. Kreml'-
        Leninu. Kopiia no. 869."

434.   Letter to Lenin, Jan. 5, 1919.
          Signed by Stalin and Dzerzhinskii, first published in P*,
        Dec. 21, 1929.
        IV, 186-189.

435.   Instruction to the Viatka Cheka, Jan. 7, 1919.
          Signed by Stalin and Dzerzhinskii, published in Gor'kov-
        skaia Kommuna, Dec. 18, 1934, according to Proletarskaia
        Revoliutsiia, p. 187. The commission of inquiry was estab-
        lished Jan. 1, consisting of Stalin and Dzerzhinskii and was
        supposed to investigate and rectify the situation on the
        Eastern Front.

436.   Telegram to Viatka Commander of the Cheka Battalion from
        the Staff of the Third Army, Jan. 7, 1919.
          Signed by Stalin and Dzerzhinskii, published in Gor'kov-
        skaia Kommuna, Dec. 18, 1934, according to Proletarskaia
        Revoliutsiia, p. 187. Evidently not the same as previous
        entry of same date.

437.   Telegram to Lenin and Central Committee, Jan. 11, 1919.
          Signed by Stalin and Dzerzhinskii, published in K 25-
        letiiu osvobozhedeniia Udmurtii ot kolchakovshchiny
        (Izhevsk, 1939), p. 17, according to Proletarskaia Revo-
        liutsiia, p. 187.

438.   Telegram to Lenin, Jan. 16, 1919.
            Signed by Stalin and Dzerzhinskii, published in K 25-
        letiiu osvobozhdeniia Udmurtii ot kolchakovshchiny (Izhevsk,
        1939), pp. 17-18, according to Proletarskaia Revoliutsiia,
        p. 187.

439.   Report to Lenin, Jan. 19, 1919.
            Signed by Stalin and Dzerzhinskii, first published in LS*,
        XXXIV, 90-93.
        IV, 190-194.

440.   Speech to Joint Party-Soviet Conference in Viatka, Jan. 19,
        1919.
            First published in Gor'kovskaia Kommuna, Dec. 18,
        1934.
        IV, 195-196.

441.   Telegram to Lenin, Jan. 23, 1919.
            Signed by Stalin and Dzerzhinskii, first published in LS*,
        XXXIV, 93-94.

442.   Report of the Commission of Inquiry of the Central Committee
        of Inquiry of the Central Committee and Soviet of Defense,
        Jan. 31, 1919.
            Signed by Stalin and Dzerzhinskii, published in P*, Jan.
        16, 1935.
        IV, 197-224.

443.   Telegram to Central Committee, Lenin, Trotsky, February 4,
        1919.
            Excerpt published in Trotsky, Stalin* (New York, Harper
        and Bros., 1941), p. 297.

444.   Telegram to the Chairman of the Ufa Revolutionary Committee,
        Feb. 6, 1919.
            Signed by Lenin and Stalin, published in ZN*, Feb. 16,
        1919.

445. Politika pravitel'stva po natsional'nomu voprosu. [The Government's Policy on the National Question.]
Signed, published in I*, Feb. 9, 1919.
IV, 225-229.

446. Sovdepam i partiinym organizatsiiam Turkestana. [To the Soviets and Party Organizations of Turkestan.]
Signed, dated Feb. 12, 1919, published in ZN*, March 2, 1919.
IV, 230-231.

447. Neobkhodimoe oproverzhenie. [A Necessary Refutation.]
Signed note in P*, Feb. 14, 1919.

448. Dva lageria. [Two Camps.]
Signed article in I*, Feb. 22, 1919.
IV, 232-235.

449. Nashi zadachi na vostoke. [Our Tasks in the East.]
Signed article in P*, March 2, 1919.
IV, 236-239.

450. Za dva goda. [Two Years.]
Signed article in ZN*, March 9, 1919.
IV, 240-244.

451. Rezervy imperializma. [Imperializm's Reserves.]
Signed article in I*, March 16, 1919.
IV, 245-248.

452. Speech at Eighth Party Congress, March 21, 1919.
Because the original account of this speech was suppressed for security reasons, the editors of the Sochineniia could only draw upon the exerpts from it that Stalin used in his speech of Aug. 1, 1927, to the Central Committee and Central Control Commission, which first appeared in Stalin's anthology Ob oppozitsii* in 1928. According to the post-Stalin edition of the Protokly of the congress, the archives of the Institute of Marxism-Leninism contain a copy of the original stenographic account of the meetings, and this was

available to the compilers of this recent edition. However, it appears that the desire to minimize Stalin's importance has led to the continued suppression of his speech. See Vos'moi s''ezd RKP(b). Protokoly (Moscow, Gos. izd. pol. lit., 1959), p. xvii.
IV, 249-250.

453.   Letter to Lenin, April 3, 1919.
        In Lenin, Ob uluchshenii gosudarstvennogo apparata i o bor'be s biurokratizmom i volokitoi (Moscow, 1930), p. 15, according to Proletarskaia Revoliutsiia, p. 139. Appears not to be the same as following entry.

454.   Report to the Supreme Central Executive Committee, April 9, 1919.
        Published in I*, April 10, 1919.
        IV, 251.

455.   K rasstrelu 26 bakinskikh tovarishchei agentami angliiskogo imperializma. [The Shooting of the Twenty-Six Baku Comrades by Agents of British Imperialism.]
        Signed article in I*, April 23.
        IV, 252-255.

456.   Draft Resolution of the Central Committee on Military Unity, May 1919.
        Signed by Lenin and Stalin, published in LS*, XXXIV, 120-121.

457.   Telegram to Antonov-Ovseenko and Podvoiskii, May 5, 1919.
        Signed by Lenin, Stalin and Krestinskii "in the name of Central Committee," published in LS*, XXXIV, 76.

458.   Telegram to Shchigry, May 7, 1919.
        Signed, first published in S.
        IV, 256-257.

459.   Telegram to L. B. Kamenev, May 8, 1919.
        Signed by Lenin, Trotsky, Stalin and Krestinskii, published in Proletarskaia Revoliutsiia*, no. 6, 1925, p. 148.

460.   Telegram to Sovnarkom of Ukraine, May 8, 1919.
        Signed by Lenin and Stalin "in the name of the Central
        Committee, " published in LS*, XXXIV, 132.

461.   Telegram to Ioffe and Rakovskii, May 9, 1919.
        Signed by Lenin, Trotsky, Krestinskii and Stalin, in the
        Trotsky Archives* of Houghton Library, Harvard University,
        item T 193.

462.   Telegram to the Staff of the Western Front, May 21, 1919.
        Signed, published in Dokumenty...Petrograda*, p. 18.

463.   Teletype Message, presumably to Staff of Western Front,
        May 24, 1919.
        Signed, published in Dokumenty...Petrograda*, pp. 19-
        20.

464.   Polozhenie o mestnykh otdeleniakh tsentral'nogo biuro zhalob
        i zaiavlenii. [Regulation of Local Departments of the Central
        Bureau of Complaints and Declarations.]
        Signed, published in I*, May 24, 1919. A detailed, official
        document on which Stalin's signature may be a formality.

465.   Teletype Message to Lenin, May 25, 1919.
        Signed, first published in Dokumenty...Petrograda*,
        pp. 19-20, which gives the date as May 24.
        IV, 258-260.

466.   Telegram to Lenin, May 28, 1919.
        Signed, published in Dokumenty...Petrograda*, p. 23.

467.   Telegram to Lenin, May 29, 1919.
        Signed by Stalin and Zinoviev, published in Dokumenty...
        Petrograda*, pp. 23-24.

468.   Teletype Message to unidentified Military Authority, pre-
        sumably in Moscow, May 30, 1919.
        Signed, published in Dokumenty...Petrograda*, p. 24.

469. K voiskam, oboroniaiushchim Petrograd! [To the Troops Defending Petrograd!]
     Signed, undated leaflet of June, 1919, published in Dokumenty...Petrograda*, p. 26.

470. Statement in Committee of Defense (Petrograd), June, 1919.
     Indirect quotations appear in Krasnaia Letopis'*, no. 3, 1934, pp. 43-45.

471. Telegram to Lenin, June 4, 1919.
     Published in Trotsky, Stalin* (New York, Harper and Bros., 1941), p. 308.

472. Telegram to Lenin, June 9, 1919.
     Signed, published in Dokumenty...Petrograda*, p. 26.

473. Telegram in Reply to Commander of First Rifle Division, June 12, 1919.
     Signed, published in Dokumenty...Petrograda*, p. 29.

474. Telegram to Lenin, June 16, 1919.
     Signed, published in P*, Dec. 21, 1929. IV, 261.

475. Teletype Message to Lenin, June 18, 1919.
     Signed, published in P*, Feb. 23, 1941. IV, 262-264.

476. Decree of Commissariat of Nationality Affairs, June 19, 1919.
     Signed, published in I*, June 19, 1919. Since Stalin was still in Petrograd when this official statement was published in Moscow, it is possible that his signature is purely formal, but not necessarily so.

477. Telegram to Lenin, June 19, 1919.
     Signed, published in Dokumenty...Petrograda*, p. 75.

478.   Telegram to the Revolutionary-Military Soviet of the Army,
         June 19, 1919.
              Signed, published in Dokumenty...Petrograda*, p. 75.

479.   Telegram to the First Rifle Division, June, 1919.
              Signed, published in Komsomol'skaia Pravda*, Feb. 22,
         1935.

480.   Telegram to Lenin, June 22, 1919.
              Unsigned, fragmentary version published in P*, Dec. 21,
         1929.

481.   Telegram to Tsiurupa, June 24, 1919.
              Signed, published in LS*, XXXIV, 180.

482.   Telegram to Lenin, June 25, 1919.
              Signed, published in Dokumenty...Petrograda*, p. 78.

483.   Telegram to the Commander of the First Rifle Division, June 28,
         1919.
              Signed by Stalin and Zinoviev, published in P*, July 1,
         1919; republished in Dokumenty...Petrograda, p. 80,
         omitting Zinoviev's signature.

484.   Telegram to Lenin, June 28, 1919.
              Unsigned, published in B*, no. 2, 1938, p. 71.

485.   O petrogradskom fronte. [The Petrograd Front.]
              Interview published in P*, July 8, 1919.
         IV, 265-271.

486.   Telegram to Lenin, July 16, 1919.
              Signed, published in LS*, XXXIV, 192-193.

487.   Order of Revolutionary-Military Soviet of Western Front, Aug. 5,
         1919.
              Signed, excerpt published in Dokumenty...Petrograda*,
         pp. 87-88.

488.   Letter to Lenin, Aug. 11, 1919.
            Signed, first published in S̲.
        IV, 272-274.

489.   Telegram to Lenin, Aug. 26, 1919.
            Signed, published in Dokumenty...Petrograda*, p. 90.

490.   Directive of Oct. 9, 1919.
            Excerpt of some order, without information on signature, a
        buted to Stalin by Voroshilov in article in P̲*, Dec. 21, 1939.

491.   Letter to Lenin, Oct. 15, 1919.
            Signed, published in P̲*, Dec. 21, 1929.
        IV, 275-277.

492.   Directive of Oct. 20, 1919.
            Attributed to Stalin by Voroshilov in article in P̲*, Dec. 21,
        1939.

493.   Undated Telegram to Lenin, 1919 (presumably autumn, while Stal
        was in Petrograd).
            Signed, in Trotsky Archives*, Houghton Library, Harvard
        University, item T 350.

494.   Telegram to Trotsky, Oct. 25, 1919.
            Signed by Stalin and Egorov, published in Petrogradskaia
        Pravda, Oct. 26, 1919. Version in S̲ states that it is addressed
        to Lenin and omits Egorov's signature.
        IV, 278.

495.   Directive, Oct. 25, 1919.
            Signed by Stalin and Ordzhonikidze, published in Orlovsko-
        kromskoe srazhenie. Skhemy boev i ob"iasneniia k nim
        (Orel, 1935), pp. 57-58, according to Proletarskaia Revoliutsi
        p. 189.

496.   Telegram to Budennyi, Oct. 28, 1919.
            Signed, published in P̲*, Nov. 19, 1939.

497.   Order to Tenth Army, Oct. 31, 1919.
            Signed, published in Pervaia konnaia (Moscow, Izogiz,
        1937), according to Proletarskaia Revoliutsiia, p. 189,
        which fails to give page no.

498.   Telegram to Lenin, Nov. 8, 1919.
            Signed, published in LS*, XXXIV, 239.

499.   Telegram to Budennyi, Nov. 19, 1919.
            Signed by Stalin and Egorov, published in Voroshilov,
        Stalin i Krasnaia Armiia* (Moscow, Voenizdat, 1937), pp.
        115-116.

500.   Speech to All-Russian Congress of Communist Organizations of
        the Peoples of the East, Nov. 22, 1919.
            First published in ZN*, Dec. 7, 1919. The following is
        omitted in S from p. 280, end of line 11: "...kotorye klialis',
        razbudit', podniat' narody Vostoka."
        IV, 279-280.

501.   Instruction to Military Commissars, Nov. 24, 1919.
            Attributed to Stalin by anonymous writer in P*, April 11,
        1938, which includes excerpt.

502.   Telegram to Voroshilov, Nov. 24, 1919.
            Excerpts from telegram attributed to Stalin by Voroshilov
        in article in P*, Dec. 21, 1939.

503.   Privetstvie Petrogradu ot iuzhnogo fronta. [Greetings to Petro-
        grad from the Southern Front.]
            Unsigned in first published version, Petrogradskaia Prav-
        da*, Dec. 18, 1919, signed in S.
        IV, 281.

504.   Telephone Message to Lenin, Dec. 23, 1919.
            Signed "Upravdel RVS Iuzhfronta," said to have been sent
        on Stalin's order, published in P*, Nov. 19, 1939.

505.   Teletype Conversation between Stalin and Egorov, on one end, and Voroshilov and Budennyi, on the other, Dec. 23-24, 1919.
      Published version in Voroshilov, Stalin i Krasnaia Armii (Moscow, Voenizdat, 1937), pp. 119-125, does not distingui between Stalin and Egorov as authors of specific portions of the conversation.

506.   K voennomu polozheniiu na Iuge. [The Military Situation in the South.]
      Signed, dated Dec. 26, 1919, published in P*, Dec. 28, 1919; postscript signed, dated Jan. 7, 1920, published in Revoliutsionnyi Front, Feb. 15, 1920.

1920

507.   Telegram, Jan. 7, 1920.
      Signed by Stalin and Egorov, published in I*, Jan. 8, 1935.

508.   Order to Southern Front, Jan. 10, 1920.
      Signed by Stalin, Egorov, Petin, published in I*, Jan. 13, 1920.

509.   Telegram to the Revolutionary Military Soviet of the Cavalry Army, Jan. 10, 1920.
      Signed by Stalin, Egorov and Petin, published in P*, Jan. 8, 1935.

510.   Telegram to Lenin, Jan. 10, 1920.
      Signed, published in P*, Jan. 8, 1935.

511.   Telegram to Lenin, Feb. 20, 1920.
      Signed, published evidently in full in Trotsky, Stalin* (New York, Harper and Bros., 1941), p. 325.

512.   Order of the Day to the Ukrainian Labor Army.
      Signed, first published in Proletarskaia Revoliutsiia, no. 3, 1940.
IV, 292-293.

513.   Statements at Fourth Conference of CP of the Ukraine, March
       17-23, 1920.

             Speech at Opening, March 17.
       IV, 294-295.

             Report on Economic Policy, March 19.
       IV, 295-302.

             Conclusion on Economic Report, March 20.
       IV, 302-303.

             Speech at Closing, March 23.
       IV, 303-304.

             Republished from records of Secretariat of Labor Army
       Staff and Kommunist (Kharkov), March 18, 21, 23, 24, 1920.

514.   Note on Draft Resolution, "not later than April 15, 1920."
       Signed, published in LS*, XXXIV, 290.

515.   Lenin, kak organizator i vozhd' RKP. [Lenin as the Organizer
       and Leader of the Russian Communist Party.]
             Signed article in P*, April 23, 1920.
       IV, 305-315.

516.   Speech at Meeting of Moscow Committee of CP, April 23, 1920.
             Published in 50-letie Vladimir Il'ich Ul'ianov-Lenin (Mos-
       cow, 1920).
       IV, 316-318.

517.   Teletype Directive to Ordzhonikidze, May 3, 1920.
             Signed by Lenin and Stalin, published in LS*, XXXIV,
       295.

518.   Telegram to Ordzhonikidze, May 5, 1920.
             Signed by Lenin and Stalin, published in Trotsky, Stalin*
       (New York, Harper and Bros., 1941), p. 266, which gives
       full text in English.

519.   Telegram to Krasin and Litvinov, May 8, 1920.
      Signed by Lenin and Stalin, published in LS*, 123-124.

520.   Instruction on Elections and Worker-Peasant Inspectorate,
      May 20, 1920.
      Signed, published in I*, May 20, 1920. An official regula-
tion on which Stalin's signature may be a formality.

521.   Memo to Lenin, May 25, 1920.
      Signed, published in LS*, XXXV, 124.

522.   Memo to Lenin, May 25, 1920.
      Signed note in series between Lenin, Stalin and Ordzhoni-
kidze, published in LS*, XXXV, 126.

523.   Novyi pokhod antanty na Rossiiu. [The Entente's New Campaign
against Russia.]
      Signed, published in P*, May 25, 26, 1920.
IV, 331-340.

524.   Telegram to Sklianskii, June 1, 1920.
      Signed, published in P*, Nov. 14, 1935.

525.   Telegram to Lenin, June 2, 1920.
      Signed, unpublished, in Trotsky Archives*, Houghton
Library, Harvard University, item T 528.

526.   Telegram to Lenin, June 3, 1920.
      Signed, unpublished, in Trotsky Archives*, Houghton
Library, Harvard University, item T 531.

527.   Telegram to Budennyi, June 3, 1920.
      Signed, published in P*, June 8, 1935.

528.   Telegram to Commanders of 12th, 14th Armies, June 8, 1920.
      Signed by Stalin and Egorov, published in P*, June 13,
1935.

529.   Telegram to Lenin, June 8, 1920.
           Signed, published in P*, Nov. 19, 1939.

530.   Message to Commanders of 12th, 13th, 14th Armies, June 9,
        1920.
           Signed by Stalin, Egorov and Pankrat'ev, first published
        in Kommunist (Kharkov), June 10, 1920; republished in P*,
        June 12, 1920.

531.   Telegram to Commander of Cavalry Army, June 10, 1920.
           Signed by Stalin and Egorov, published in P*, June 12,
        1935.

532.   Telegram to Commander of Thirteenth Army, June 10, 1920.
           Signed by Egorov, Stalin and Pankrat'ev, published in
        P*, Nov. 14, 1935.

533.   Letter to Lenin, June 12, 1920.
           Signed, published in Lenin, Sochineniia*, 3rd ed., XXV,
        624.

534.   Telegram to Commanders of 13th and 14th Armies, June 13,
        1920.
           Signed by Stalin and Egorov, published in Voroshilov,
        Stalin i Krasnaia Armiia* (Moscow, Voenizdat, 1937), pp.
        153-154.

535.   Telegram to Commander, First Cavalry Army, June 13, 1920.
           Signed by Stalin and Egorov, published in Voroshilov,
        Stalin i Krasnaia Armiia* (Moscow, Voenizdat, 1937), p.
        153.

536.   Letter to Revolutionary Military Committee of the CP, June 17,
        1920.
           Attributed to Stalin by Voroshilov in article in P*, Dec.
        21, 1939, including excerpts but no information on signature.

537.   Telegram to Lenin, June 19, 1920.
           Signed, published in P*, Nov. 19, 1939.

538.   O polozhenii na iugo-zapadnom fronte. [The Situation on the
        South-Western Front.]
            Interview in Kommunist (Kharkov), June 24, 1920.
        IV, 329-334.

539.   Telegram to Lenin, June 25, 1920.
            Signed, published in P*, Nov. 14, 1935.
        IV, 335.

540.   Greetings to First Cavalry Army, June 27, 1920.
            Unsigned, attributed to Stalin by P*, Nov. 19, 1939,
        which publishes text.

541.   Telegram to Lenin, July 1, 1920.
            Signed, published in P*, Nov. 14, 1935.

542.   Telegram to Commander of 31th Army, July 1, 1920.
            Signed by Stalin, Egorov and Libus, published in P*,
        Nov. 14, 1935.

543.   Telegram to Lenin, July 2, 1920.
            Signed, published in P*, Nov. 14, 1935. Mainly a cover-
        ing letter for material from a White newspaper.

544.   Telegram to the Revolutionary Military Soviet (Moscow),
        July 3, 1920.
            Signed, published in LS*, XXXIV, 333.

545.   Telegram to Lenin, July 5, 1920.
            Signed, published in LS*, XXXIV, 333-334.

546.   Telegram to Glavkom and Revolutionary Military Soviet (Mos-
        cow), July 5, 1920.
            Signed, published in LS*, XXXIV, 334.

547.   Letter to Editor of Pravda.
            Signed, published in P*, July 9, 1920.

548.   Letter to Lenin, July 11, 1920.
            Signed, published in LS*, XXXIV, 335.

549.   O polozhenii na pol'skom fronte. [The Situation on the Polish
        Front.]
            Interview in P*, June 11, 1920.
        IV, 336-341.

550.   Kak vstrechaiut krasnye voiska. [How the Red Army Is Greeted.]
            Interview in Krasnoarmeets, July 15, 1920.
        IV, 342-343.

551.   Draft Letter to the Central Committee, "July, 1920."
            Unsigned, first published in LS*, XXXV, 140.
        IV, 344-345.

552.   Telegram to Lenin, July 18.
            Signed, published in LS*, XXXVI, 110-111.

553.   Telegram to Deputy Chairman of Revolutionary Military Soviet
        (Moscow), July 24, 1920.
            Signed, published in P*, Nov. 14, 1935.

554.   Telegram to Presidium of Supreme Central Executive Committee,
        no later than Aug. 1, 1920.
            Published in Iz istorii partiinogo stroitel'stva v Kazakh-
        stane. Sbornik statei.* (Alma Ata, Kazakhstanskoe kraevoe
        izd., 1936), p. 225. Cites archival source and makes definite
        identification of Stalin as author.

555.   Directive to the Command of the Southwestern Front, Aug. 1,
        1920.
            Signed, published in S. Borisov, M.F. Frunze* (Moscow,
        Voenizdat, 1940), p. 212.

556.   Telegram to Lenin, Aug. 3, 1920.
            Signed, published in LS*, XXXVI, 115-116.

557. Telegram to Commander of 13th Army, Aug. 6, 1920.
          Signed by Stalin and Egorov, published in P*, Nov. 14,
      1935.

558. Telegram to Lenin, Aug. 7, 1920.
          Signed, published in P*, Nov. 14, 1935.

559. Telegram to Lenin, Aug. 10, 1920.
          Signed, published in LS*, XXXIV, 343.

560. Teletype Directive to Central Committee of Ukrainian CP,
      Aug. 19, 1920.
          Signed by Lenin and Stalin, published in LS*, XXXIV,
      348.

561. Teletype Directive to Caucasian Bureau of Central Committee,
      Aug. 19, 1920.
          Signed by Lenin and Stalin, published in LS*, XXXIV,
      348-349.

562. Teletype Directive to Siberian Bureau of Central Committee,
      Aug. 19, 1920.
          Signed by Lenin and Stalin, published in LS*, XXXIV, 349.

563. Memo to Politburo, Aug. 20, 1930.
          Signed, published in LS*, XXXIV, 145.

564. Ko vsem soldatam i ofitseram armii Vrangelia. [To All Soldiers
      and Officers of Vrangel's Army.]
          Article signed by Stalin and Egorov in Izvestiia Ekaterino-
      slavskogo Gubernskogo Ispolkoma, Aug. 22, 1920. Repub-
      lished in Voroshilov, Stalin i Krasnaia Armiia* (Moscow,
      Voenizdat, 1937), pp. 159-163. Although Stalin was in Mos-
      cow when this was published in Ekaterinoslav, some passages
      in it are very like parts of his article in S, IV, 282-291.
      Perhaps this earlier article by Stalin was rewritten by other
      hands and his signatures were again used to lend authority.

565. Memo to Politburo, Aug. 25, 1920.
      Signed, first published in S̲.
   IV, 346-348.

566. Memo to Politburo, Aug. 30, 1920
      Signed, first published in S̲.
   IV, 348-350.

567. Memo to Lenin, Sept. 7, 1920.
      Signed, published in LS̲*, XXXV, 149.

568. Politika sovetskoi vlasti po natsional'nomu voprosu v Rossii.
   [The Policy of the Soviet Government on the National Question
   in Russia.]
      Signed article in P̲*, Oct. 10, 1920.
   IV, 351-363.

569. Speech to First All-Russian Conference of Responsible Personnel of the Workers' and Peasants' Inspection, Oct. 15, 1920.
      First published in Izvestiia Raboche-Krestianskoi In-
     spektsii, Nov.-Dec., 1920.
   IV, 364-369.

570. Preface to Sbornik statei (by Stalin).
      Anthology published: Tula, Giz, 1920.
   IV, 370-373.

571. Telegram to Central Committee, Oct. 26, 1920.
      Signed, published in LS̲*, XXXIV, 373.

572. Speech to Regional Conference of Communist Organizations of
   the Don and Caucasus, Oct. 27, 1920.
      First published in Kommunist (Vladikavkaz), Oct. 30, 1920.
   IV, 374-381.

573. Memo to Lenin, November, 1920.
      Signed, published in LS̲*, XXXV, 175-176.

574. Speech to Baku Soviet, Nov. 6, 1920.
First published in Kommunist (Baku), Nov. 7 and 11,
1920.
IV, 382-393.

575. Speech to the Congress of the Peoples of Daghestan, Nov. 13,
1920.
First published in Sovetskii Dagestan, Nov. 17, 1920.
Republished in ZN*, Dec. 15, 1920.
IV, 394-398.

576. Speech to Congress of the Peoples of the Terek Region, Nov. 17
1920.
First published in ZN*, Dec. 8, 15, 1920.
IV, 399-407.

577. Teletype Conversation with Lenin, "not later than Nov. 20,
1920."
Signed, published in LS*, XXXIV, 175.

578. Polozhenie na Kavkaze. [The Situation in the Caucasus.]
Interview published in P*, Nov. 30, 1920.
IV, 408-412.

579. Da zdravstvuet sovetskaia Armeniia! [Long Live Soviet Armenia
Signed article in P*, Dec. 4, 1920.
IV, 413-444.

1921

580. Speech at Conference of the Tiurk Peoples, Jan. 1, 1921.
In P*, Jan. 12, 1921. P. 2, lines 7-8: "esli ne schitat'
nekotorykh nastroenii k 'velikoderzhavnomu shovinizmu"
have been interpolated.
V, 1-3.

581. Nashi raznoglasiia. [Our Disagreements.]
Signed article in P*, Jan. 19, 1921. P. 7, following line
18, omits: "sm. 'Chernovoi Nabrosok Tezisov' T. Trotskogo
o profsoiuzakh, razoslannyi chlenam Ts. K. v noiabre."
V, 4-14.

582.   Speech to Soviet of Nationalities, Jan. 19, 1921.
        Direct quotation and additional indirect quotation appears
        in E. B. Genkina, Obrazovanie SSSR* (Moscow, Ogiz, 1946),
        p. 79.

583.   Ob ocherednykh zadachakh partii v natsional'nom voprose.
        [The Immediate Tasks of the Party in the National Question.]
            Theses for Tenth Party Congress, published in P*, Feb.
        10, 1921. P. 20, line 17, should include "v Finliandii, "
        following "Bavarii." On pp. 27-28 the word "tuzemtsy" has
        been replaced by the expression "mestnye korennye zhiteli."
        V, 15-29.

584.   Statements at Tenth Party Congress, March 8-16, 1921.

            Report on the National Question, March 10. At numerous
        places "tuzemtsy" has been replaced by "mestnye korennye
        zhiteli."
        V, 33-44.

            Conclusion on the National Question, March 10.
        V, 45-49.

            Published in Desiatyi s"ezd Rossiiskoi Kommunisticheskoi
        Partii. Stenograficheskii otchet.* (Petrograd: Gos. izd.,
        1921).

585.   Letter to Lenin, March 1921.
            Signed, first published in Stalin. Sbornik statei k piatdesia-
        tiletiiu so dnia rozhdeniia (Moscow, 1929).
        V, 50-51.

586.   K postanovke national'nogo voprosa. [Concerning the Presenta-
        tion of the National Question.]
            Signed, date May 2, published in P*, May 8, 1921.
        V, 52-59.

587.   Letter to the Chairman of the Congress of Soviets of the Kabard
        District, June 12, 1921.
            Signed, published in Krasnaia Kabarda (Nal'chik), no. 7,
        republished in N. Izgoev, Rasskaz o Kabarde (Moscow,
        Molodaia Gvardia, 1936), pp. 14-15, according to Proletarskaia
        Revoliutsiia.

588.   Greeting to First Congress of Mountaineer Women, June 17, 1921.
        Signed first published in Biulleten' I s''ezda trudovykh zhenshchin Vostoka Gorskoi Sovetskoi Sotsialisticheskoi Respubliki (Vladikavkaz, 1921).
        V, 60-61.

589.   O politicheskoi strategii i taktike russkikh kommunistov. [The Political Strategy and Tactics of the Russian Communists.]
        Rough draft, dated July, 1921, first published in S. See editorial note V, 87, on relation of this draft to later essays V, 62-87.

590.   Ob ocherednykh zadachakh kommunizma v Gruzii i Zakavkaz'e. [The Immediate Tasks of Communism in Georgia and Trans-caucasia.]
        Speech of July 6, 1921, first published in Pravda Gruzii*, July 13, 1921.
        V, 88-100.

591.   Partiia do i posle vziatiia vlasti. [The Party before and after Taking Power.]
        Signed article in P*, Aug. 28, 1921.
        V, 101-112.

592.   Memo to Lenin, Aug. 31, 1921.
        Signed, published in LS*, XXXV, 219.

593.   Telegram to Narimanov, Sept. 26, 1921.
        Signed by Lenin and Stalin, published in LS*, XXXV, 280.

594.   Letter to Lenin, Sept. 27, 1921.
        Signed, published in Lenin, Sochineniia*, 3rd ed., XXVII, p. 501.

595.   Memo to Lenin, Oct. 20, 1921.
        Signed, published in LS*, XXXV, 278.

596.   Oktiabr'skaia revoliutsiia i natsional'naia politika russkikh
        kommunistov. [The October Revolution and the National Policy
        of the Russian Communists.]
            Signed, published in P*, Nov. 6, 7, 1921.
        V, 113-116.

597.   Memo to Lenin, Nov. 22, 1921.
            Signed, published LS*, XXXV, 295.

598.   Letter to Lenin, Nov. 22, 1921.
            Signed, published in LS*, XXXIV, 427.

599.   Perspektivy. [The Prospects.]
            Signed article in P*, Dec. 18, 1921. The following open-
        ing passage has been omitted from S: "Pokhod mezhdunarodnoi
        burzhuazii protiv Sovetskoi Rossii prinial formu skrytoi
        bor'by. Nesmotria na ustanovivsheesia nekotoroe ravnovesie,
        burzhuaziia prodolzhaet gotovit'sia k napadeniiam. Neobkhodi-
        ma bditel'nost'. Voennyi soiuz rabochikh i krest'ian dal nam
        pobedu v proshlom. Khoziaistvennyi soiuz rabochikh i
        krest'ian sdelaet nas nesokrushimymi. Uspekhi na khoziaist-
        vennom fronte--luchshaia garantiia prochnosti etogo soiuza."
        V, 117-127.

                        1922

600.   Memo to Lenin, Jan. 6, 1922.
            Signed, published in LS*, XXXV, 311.

601.   Memo to Lenin, Jan. 12, 1922.
            Signed, published in LS*, XXXV, 312.

602.   Memo to Molotov, Jan. 14, 1922.
            Signed, published in LS*, XXXV, 315.

603.   Note on Letter from Lenin to Ordzhonikidze, Feb. 13, 1922.
            Signed, published in Lenin, Sochineniia*, 3rd ed., XXVII,
        517-518.

604.   Memorandum to Molotov (as Member of Secretariat of Central
        Committee). March 10, 1922.
            Signed by Stalin and Kamenev, unpublished, in Trotsky
        Archives*, Houghton Library, Harvard University, item
        T 735.

605.   "Pravde." [To Pravda.]
            Signed article in P*, May 5, 1922.
        V, 128.

606.   K desiatiletiiu "Pravdy." Vospominaniia.
        [The Tenth Anniversary of Pravda. Reminiscences.]
            Signed article in P*, May 5, 1922.
        V, 129-133.

607.   Letter to Executive Committee of the Comintern.
            Signed, published in P*, May 19, 1922.

608.   Letter to the Communists of the Kirghiz Republic, May 20, 1922.
            Signed, published in ZN*, June 15, 1922.

609.   Notice of Meeting of Aug. 3, 1922.
            Signed, published in P*, July 8, 1922. A formal notice
        sent to all guberniia and oblast' committees of the CP, to
        national central committees, krai committees, to political
        departments of armies, military okrugs and fronts.

610.   Directive to Guberniia Committees, National Central Commit-
        tees, Oblast' Bureaus of Central Committees, July 8, 1922.
            Signed, formal directive, published in P*, July 9, 1922.

611.   Tov. Lenin na otdykhe. Zametki. [Comrade Lenin on Vacation.
        Notes.]
            Article in P*, Sept. 24, 1922, ill. supplement. Signed
        Sept. 15, 1922.
        V, 134-136.

612.   Letter to Lenin, Sept. 27, 1922.
            Partially published in Trotsky, Stalinskaia shkola

fal'shivikatsii (Berlin, Izdatel'stvo "Granit, " 1932), pp. 66-
67. Full document in Trotsky Archives*, Houghton Library,
Harvard University, item T 755. The essence of this letter
as given in the Trotsky Archives is confirmed by V.V.
Pentkovskaia in "Rol' V.I. Lenina v obrazovanii SSR, "
Voprosy Istorii, 1956, no. 3, pp. 13-24.

613. Telegram to Central Committee of CP of Georgia, Oct. 16,
1922.
       Quoted, evidently in full, by Beria, p. 245, which cites
archives of Georgian CP and makes definite attributions to
Stalin.

614. Greetings to Petrograd Soviet.
       Signed, published in Petrogradskaia Pravda*, Nov. 5,
1922.
V, 137.

615. Vopros ob ob''edinenii nezavisimykh natsional'nykh respublik.
[The Question of the Union of the Independent National Republics.]
       Interview published in P*, Nov. 18, 1922. P. 141, last
line, "shovinizma" should read "patriotizma." P. 143, line
30, "pri nalichii verkhnei palaty" has been added in S. P. 144,
last two lines, "pokushenii so storony mezhdunarodnogo" has
been added in S.
V, 138-144.

616. Ob ob''edinenii sovetskikh respublik. [The Unification of the
Soviet Republics.]
       Speech to Tenth All-Russian Congress of Soviets, Dec. 26,
1922, published in P*, Dec. 28, 1922. P. 150, line 29,
"nemtsami, evreiami" should appear following "ukraintsami."
P. 155, line 23, "mirovuiu" should read "edinuiu."
V, 145-155.

617. Ob obrazovanii soiuza sovetskikh sotsialisticheskikh respublik.
[The Formation of the Union of Soviet Socialist Republics.]
       Speech to the First Congress of Soviets of the USSR, Dec.
30, 1922, published in P*, Dec. 31, 1922. P. 156, line 19,
following "vlast' " omits: "razrushiv stariiu armiiu, ne
uspela eshche sozdat' novuiu..." The last four paragraphs
on p. 159 do not appear in P.
V, 156-159.

1923

618. K voprosu o strategii i taktike russkikh kommunistov. [Con-
cerning the Question of the Strategy and Tactics of the Russian
Communists.]
      Signed, published in P*, March 14, 1923.
V, 160-180.

619. Natsional'nye momenty v partiinom i gosudarstvennom stroitel'
stve. [National Factors in Party and State Affairs.]
      Theses for Twelfth Party Congress, signed published in
      P*.
V, 181-194.

620. Declaration to Central Committee, April 16, 1923.
      Signed, published in English in The Department of State
Bulletin, XXXV, no. 891 (1956), p. 161.

621. Statements at Twelfth Party Congress, April 17-25, 1923.

      Organization Report, April 17.
V, 197-222.

      Conclusion on Organization Report, April 19.
V, 223-235.

      Report on the National Question, April 23. P. 246, follow
ing line 30, S omits: "Takov pervyi i samyi opasnyi faktor
tormoziashchii dela ob'edineniia narodov i respublik v edinyi
soiuz."
V, 236-263.

      Conclusion on the National Question, April 25.
V, 264-275.

      Reply to Proposed Amendments to Resolution on National
Question, April 25.
V, 276-278.

      Supplement to Report on the National Question, April 25.
V, 279-280.

Statement in Discussion, April 25. Stenograficheskii otchet, p. 607.

All of above published in Dvenadtsatyi s''ezd RKP(b). Stenograficheskii otchet* (Moscow, Krasnaia nov', 1923).

622.   Pechat' kak kollektivnyi organizator. [The Press as a Collective Organizer.]
        Signed article in P*, May 6, 1923.
V, 281-285.

623.   Chem dal'she v les... [Confusion Worse Confounded.]
        Signed article in P*, May 10, 1923.
V, 286-290.

624.   Statements at Fourth Conference of the Central Committee with Responsible Workers of National Republics and Regions, June 9-12, 1923.

        Draft Platform on the National Question.
V, 293-300.

        Speech of June 10 on First Item of Agenda.
V, 301-312.

        Speech of June 10 on Second Item of Agenda.
V, 313-326.

        Conclusion, June 12.
V, 327-339.

        Answer to Discussion, June 12.
V, 340-341.

        All of above published in Chetvertoe soveshchanie TsK RKP s otvetstvennymi rabotnikami natsional'nyk respublik i oblastei. Stenograficheskii otchet. (Moscow, 1923).

625.   Letter to Bukharin and Zinoviev, Aug., 1923.
        Published, evidently in full, in English, in Trotsky, Stalin (New York: Harper and Bros., 1941), pp. 368-369.

626.   Letter to Thalheimer, Oct. 1923.
             Signed, published in German in <u>Die Rote Fahne</u>*, Oct. 10
         1923.

627.   Oktiabr'skaia revoliutsiia i vopros o srednikh sloiakh. [The
         October Revolution and the Question of the Middle Strata.]
             Signed article in <u>P</u>*, Nov. 7, 1923.
         V, 342-348.

628.   K piatoi godovshchine Pervogo S'ezda Rabotnits i Krest'ianok.
         [The Fifth Anniversary of the First Congress of Working
         Women and Peasant Women.]
             Signed article in <u>Kommunistka</u>, no. 11, Nov., 1923, p. 1.
         V, 349-351.

629.   Speech at Military Academy, Nov. 17, 1923.
             Published in <u>I</u>*, Nov. 20, 1923.
         V, 352-353.

630.   O zadachakh partii. [The Tasks of the Party.] Dec. 2, 1923.
             Speech to Krasnaia Presnia raion committee of the party,
         published in <u>P</u>*, Dec. 6, 1923.
         V, 354-370.

631.   Notice to all CP organizations, Dec. 14, 1923.
             Signed, published in <u>P</u>*, Dec. 15, 1923.

632.   O diskussii, o Tov. Rafaile, o stat'iakh Tt. Preobrazhenskogo
         i Sapronova i o pis'me Tov. Trotskogo. [The Discussion,
         Comrade Rafail, the Articles by Comrades Preobrazhenskii
         and Sapronov, and Comrade Trotsky's Letter.]
             Signed article published in <u>P</u>*, Dec. 15, 1923. In <u>S</u> the
         address "tovarishch" is dropped in referring to those indi-
         cated in the title, as is always the case with persons who
         later became "enemies of the people." On pp. 272-273
         references to published works by Preobrazhenskii are
         omitted in <u>S</u>.
         V, 371-387.

633.   Neobkhodimoe zamechanie. [A Necessary Comment.]
         Signed article in P*, Dec. 28, 1923.
      V, 388-391.

634.   Greeting to Kommunist.
         Signed, published in Bakinskii Rabochii, Dec. 30, 1923.
      V, 392.

                              1924

635.   Greeting to Kommunist (Baku).
         Signed, published in Zaria Vostoka, Jan. 3, 1924,
      according to Proletarskaia Revoliutsiia, p. 195.

636.   O diskussii. [The Discussion.]
         Interview dated Jan. 9, 1924, published in Zaria Vostoka,
      Jan. 10, 1924.
      VI, 1-2.

637.   Statements at Thirteenth Party Conference, Jan. 16-18, 1924.

         Report on Party Affairs, Jan. 17.
      V, 5-26.

         Conclusion, Jan. 18.
      VI, 25-45.

         P. 30, line 31, should include: "Preobrazhenskii: 'Esli
      Pravda napechataet.' Stalin: 'Konechno napechataet.'" Also
      interjection by Riazanov, p. 42, line 2 and interjection from
      unidentified delegate, p. 44, line 2. P. 45, line 15, follow-
      ing "Ivanovich" S omits: "Redaktor etogo organa pobyval v
      marksistskoi shkole i, khotia ushel ot marksistov, ostatki
      starogo chut'ia eshche sohranilis' u nego. Eto byvshii
      marksist sviazannyi so II Internatsionalom."

         All of above published in Trinadtsataia konferentsiia
      Rossiiskoi kommunisticheskoi partii (bol'shevikov).
      Biulleten'. (Moscow, 1924) and P*, Jan. 20, 22, 1924.

638.   Po povodu smerti Lenina. [On the Death of Lenin.]
        Speech to the Second All-Union Congress of Soviets,
        Jan. 26, 1924, published in P*, Jan. 30, 1924.
        VI, 46-51.

639.   O Lenine. [Lenin.]
        Speech to Kremlin Military School, Jan. 28, 1924, pub-
        lished in P*, Feb. 12, 1924. P. 59, line 15, "sotsial-
        patsifizma" added in S. P. 64, lines 1-6, should read, in
        place of version in S: "Etim ia konchaiu, tovarishchi, svoiu
        rech'. Nechego i govorit', chto ia ne ischerpal i desiatoi
        doli tekh vospominanii o kotorykh sledovalo by vam rass-
        kazat'. No ogranichimsia poka skazannym, otlozhiv otstal'noe
        do sleduiushchego raza."
        V 52-64.

640.   Ob Institute V.I. Lenina. [The V.I. Lenin Institute.]
        Appeal for Leniniana, signed by Stalin and L. Kamenev,
        published in Proletarskaia Revoliutsiia, no. 1, 1924, p. 311.

641.   O protivorechiiakh v Komsomole. [On the Contradictions in the
        Komsomol.]
        Speech to conference on party work among the youth,
        April 3, 1924, published in Lenin and Stalin, O Komsomole*
        (Moscow, 1926).
        VI, 65-68.

642.   Speech to Orgburo, April 6, 1924.
        In Lenin and Stalin, O Molodezhi* (Moscow, Partizdat,
        1936), pp. 169-174.

643.   Ob osnovakh leninizma. [The Foundations of Leninism.]
        Lectures at Sverdlov University, first published in P*,
        April 26, 30; May 9, 11, 14, 15, 18, 1924. P. 107, lines
        19-29, should read: "...pobedu sotsializma. Glavnaia
        zadacha sotsializma--organizatsiia sotsialisticheskogo
        proizvodstva--ostaetsia eshche vperedi. Mozhno li razreshit'
        etu zadachu, mozhno li dobit'sia okonchatel'noi pobedy
        sotsializma v odnoi strane, bez sovmestnykh usilii prole-
        tariev neskol'kikh stran? Net, nevozmozhno. Dlia sverzheniia
        burzhuazii dostatochno usilii odnoi strany--ob etom govorit

nam istoriia nashei revoliutsii. Dlia okonchatel'noi pobedy
sotsializma, dlia organizatsii sotsialisticheskogo proiz-
vodstva, usilii odnoi strany, osobeno takoi krest'ianskoi
strany kak Rossiia, uzhe ne dostatochno--dlia etogo neob-
khodimy usiliia proletariev neskol'kikh peredovykh stran.
Poetomu razvitie..." The alteration of this original formula-
tion occurred shortly after publication and not at the time
of the compilation of S.
VI, 69-188.

644.   Plan seminarii po leninizmu. [Plan for a Seminar on Leninism.]
          Signed, published in Krasnaia Molodezh*, no. 1, 1924,
       pp. 4-8.

645.   Telegram to Baltic Fleet, May, 1924.
          Signed, published in Krasnyi Baltiiskii Flot, July 9, 1939,
       according to Proletarskaia Revoliutsiia, p. 196.

646.   Statements at Thirteenth Party Congress, May 23-31, 1924.

          Organizational Report, May 24.
       VI, 191-219.

          Conclusion, May 27.
       VI, 220-233.

          S relies on version in P*, May 27, 28, instead of steno-
       graphic report, as is its usual practice. However, the two
       texts seem to agree on Stalin's contributions. See Trinadtsatyi
       s''ezd Rossiiskoi Kommunisticheskoi partii (bol'shevikov).
       Stenograficheskii otchet* (Moscow, 1924).

647.   Ob itogakh XIII s''ezda RKP(b). [The Results of the Thirteenth
       Congress of the RCP(b).] June 17, 1924.
          Speech to class for uezd party secretaries, published in
          P*, June 19, 20, 1924.
       VI, 234-260.

648.   O rabkorakh. [Worker Correspondents.]
          Signed interview in Rabochii Korrespondent, no. 6, 1924.
       VI, 261-263.

649.　O kompartii Pol'shi. [The Polish Communist Party.] July 3, 19
　　　　Speech to the Polish Commission of the Comintern, [5th
　　Congress] published in B*, no. 11, 1924, pp. 51-55.
　　VI, 264-272.

650.　Letter to Demian Bednyi, July 15, 1924.
　　　　Signed, first published in S.
　　VI, 273-276.

651.　O Ia. M. Sverdlove. [Ia. M. Sverdlov.]
　　　　Article signed Aug. 2, 1924, in Proletarskaia Revoliutsiia
　　no. 11, 1924.
　　VI, 277-279.

652.　K mezhdunarodnomu polozheniiu. [Concerning the International
　　Situation.]
　　　　Article signed Sept. 12, in P* Sept. 20, 1924.
　　VI, 280-301.

653.　Greeting to Youth Correspondents, Oct. 20, 1924.
　　　　Signed in Raboche-krest'ianskii korrespondent, no. 10,
　　1934, according to Proletarskaia Revoliutsiia, p. 196.

654.　Letter to Youth Corresondent Maksimov, Oct. 20, 1924. [2 notes
　　　　Signed, published in Raboche-krest'ianskii korrespondent,
　　no. 10, 1924, according to Proletarskaia Revoliutsiia, p. 196

655.　Ob ocherednykh zadachakh partii v derevne. [The Party's
　　Immediate Tasks in the Countryside.]
　　　　Speech to conference of secretaries of rural party organi-
　　zations, Oct. 22, 1920, published in P*, Oct. 23, 1924.
　　VI, 302-312.

656.　O zadachakh partii v derevne. [The Party's Tasks in the
　　Countryside.]
　　　　Speech to Central Committee Plenum, Oct. 26, 1924, pub-
　　lished in Stalin, Krest'ianskii vopros* (Moscow, Gosizdat,
　　1925), pp. 33-40.
　　VI, 313-320

657.   Note in "Dinamo" Factory Visitors' Book, Nov. 7, 1924.
            Signed, published in P*, June 4, 1930.
        VI, 321.

658.   Greeting to First Cavalry Army. Nov. 15, 1924.
            Signed, published in P*, Nov. 16, 1924.
        VI, 322.

659.   Greeting to Krest'ianskaia Gazeta.
            Signed, published in Krest'ianskaia Gazeta*, Nov. 17,
        1924.
        VI, 323.

660.   Letter to Central Committee of German CP.
            Signed on behalf of Central Committee of Russian CP,
        published in P*, Nov. 18, 1924.

661.   Trotskizm ili leninism? [Trotskyism or Leninism?]
            Speech to Communist delegation to A.U.C.C.T.U.,
        Nov. 19, 1924, published in P*, Nov. 26, 1924.
        VI, 324-357.

662.   Oktiabr'skaia revoliutsiia i taktika russkikh kommunistov.
        [The October Revolution and the Tactics of the Russian Com-
        munists.]
            Preface, dated Dec. 17, to Stalin anthology Na putiakh k
        Oktiabriu (Moscow, G12, 1925), pp. vii-lvi. Portions of
        this preface (pp. ix-xii in part) appear in S, III, 28-31 (see
        No. 151). However, other portions of the beginning of this
        essay in its original version have been entirely omitted from
        S, and are reproduced in appendix C.
        VI, 358-401.

                            1925

663.   Rabotnitsy i krest'ianki, pomnite i vypolniaite zavety Il'icha!
        [Working Women and Peasant Women, Remember and Carry
        Out Ilyich's Behests!]
            Signed article in Rabotnitsa, Jan. 5, 1925.
        VII, 1-2.

                            113

664.   Uchitel'skomu s"ezdu. [To the Teachers' Congress.]
            Article signed Jan. 6, 1925, published in Uchitel'skaia
       Gazeta, Jan. 10, 1925.
       VII, 3.

665.   O zadachakh zhurnala Krasnaia Molodezh'. [The Tasks of the
       Magazine Krasnaia Molodezh'.]
            Interview in Krasnaia Molodezh', Jan., 1925.
       VII, 4-5.

666.   Speech to the Central Committee and Central Control Commis-
       sion, Jan. 17, 1924.
            Published in pamphlet O trotskizme* (Moscow, 1925).
       VII, 6-10.

667.   Speech to Central Committee, Jan. 19, 1925.
            First published in S.
       VII, 11-14.

668.   Note in Rabochaia Gazeta.
            Signed, published in Rabochaia Gazeta, Jan. 21, 1925.
       VII, 15.

669.   Letter to D--ov, Jan. 25, 1925.
            First published in S.
       VII, 16-18.

670.   O "Dymovke." ["Dymovka".]
            Speech to Orgburo, Jan. 26, 1925, published in Stalin,
       Krest'ianskii vopros* (Moscow: Gosizdat, 1925), pp. 47-55.
       VII, 19-24.

671.   K voprosu o proletariate i krest'ianstve. [Concerning the Ques-
       tion of the Proletariat and the Peasantry.]
            Speech to 13th Guberniia Conference of Moscow Party
       Organization, Jan. 27, 1925, published in P*, Jan. 30, 1925.
       VII, 25-33.

672.   O perspektivakh KPG i o bol'shevizatsii. [The Prospects of the
        CPG and Bolshevization.]
                Interview, Feb. 3, 1925, with Herzog, member of the
            C.P.G., published in P*, Feb. 3, 1925.
        VII, 34-41.

673.   Letter to Pravda Vostoka (Tashkent) for transmission to the
        Party Kurultai of Uzbekistan.
                Signed, published in Pravda Vostoka (Tashkent), Feb. 6, 1925.

674.   Greeting to First Party Congress of CP of Turkmenia.
                First published in Turkmenskaia Iskra, Feb. 14, 1925;
            republished in I*, Nov. 24, 1939.

675.   Letter to Me--rt (Maslow), Feb. 28, 1925.
                Although S states that this is the first publication of this
            document, it was in fact first published in German (translated
            from the Russian) in Die Aktion, vol. XVI, no. 9, Sept.,
            1926, according to Rush Fischer, Stalin and German Com-
            munism (Cambridge, Harvard University Press, 1948), p.
            435. Fischer gives an English translation from the German,
            pp. 435-439, which differs only slightly from the version in
            S. She states that Arkady Maslow was the original addressee.
        VII, 42-47.

676.   K mezhdunarodnomu zhenskomu dniu. [International Women's
        Day.]
                Signed article in P*, March 8, 1925.
        VII, 48-49.

677.   Greeting to First Party Congress of Tadzhikistan.
                Signed, published in Pravda Vostoka (Tashkent), March
            12, 1925.*

678.   Letter to the Central Executive Committee of the Kuomintang.
                Signed Mar. 13, 1925 on behalf of Central Committee,
            published in P*, March 14, 1925.
        VII, 50-51.

679.   Interview with Bednota Correspondent, March 14, 1925.
        Published in Bednota, April 5, 1925. In his report to the
        Fourteenth Party Congress (S, VII, 363) Stalin denied the reli
        bility of this published version.

680.   Greeting to the Party Conference of Kara-Kirghizia, March 14,
        Signed, published in Pravda Vostoka (Tashkent), March 26
        1925.*

681.   K mezhdunarodnomu polozheniiu i zadacham kompartii. [The Inte
        national Situation and the Tasks of Communist Parties.]
        Signed article in P*, March 22, 1925.
        VII, 52-58.

682.   O chekhoslovatskoi kompartii. [The Communist Party of Czecho-
        slovakia.]
        Speech to the Czechoslovak Commission of the Comintern
        Executive Committee, March 27, 1925, [5th Plenum] pub-
        lished in P*, March 29, 1925.
        VII, 59-68.

683.   K natsional'nomu voprosu Iugoslavii. [Concerning the National Q
        tion in Yugoslavia.]
        Speech to the Yugoslav Commission of the Comintern Exec
        Committee, March 30, 1925, published in B*, no. 7, 1925, p
        20-23.
        VII, 69-76.

684.   Speech to Czechoslovak Commission of Executive Committee of
        Comintern, March 30, 1925. [5th Plenum]
        Published in Kommunisticheskii Internatsional*, no. 4, 19
        pp. 45-47.

685.   Greeting to the Azerbaidjainian CP.
        Signed, published in Bakinskii Proletarii, April 5, 1925; r
        lished in article by M. Bagirov in P*, Dec. 30, 1935.

686.   O komsomol'skom aktive v derevne. [The Activists of the Komso
        in the Countryside.]
        Speech to Orgburo, April 6, 1925, published in P*, April 1
        1925.
        VII, 77-84.

687.   Letter to editor of Bednota, ca. April 10.
         VII, 363 (read by Stalin in the conclusion on the political report
         to the Twelfth Party Congress).

688.   Message to the First All-Union Conference of Proletarian Students,
         April 15.
              Signed, published in P*, April 16, 1925.
         VII, 85-89.

689.   K itogam rabot XIV konferentsii RKP(b). [The Results of the Work of
         the Fourteenth Conference of the RCP(b).]
              Speech to the activists of the Moscow party organization, May 9,
              1925, published in P*, May 12, 13, 1925.
         VII, 90-132.

690.   O politicheskikh zadachakh universiteta narodov vostoka. [The Politi-
         cal Tasks of the University of the Peoples of the East.]
              Speech to students at the Communist University of the Toilers
              of the East, May 18, 1925, published in P*, May 22, 1925. P. 146,
              line 27, "bor'ba" should read "voina." P. 147, line 7, omits "kak
              gomindana" after "...partii raboche-krest'ianskoi."
         VII, 133-152.

691.   Letter to the Editors of Komsomolskaia Pravda, June 2, 1925.
              Signed by Stalin, Molotov, Andreev, first published in full
              in S. Excerpts published in Chetyrnadtsatyi s''ezd VKP(b),
              Stenografi-cheskii otchet. (Moscow: gos. izd., 1926), pp.
              204-205, 504.
         VII, 153-155.

692.   Speech at Sverdlov University, June 9, 1925.
              Published in P*, June 21, 24, 25, 28, 1925.
         VII, 156-211.

693.   Message to Sverdlov University.
              Signed, published in P*, June 13, 1925.
         VII, 212-215.

694.   Eshche raz k natsional'nomu voprosu. [The National Question
         Once Again.]
              Signed article in B*, no. 11-12, 1925.
         VII, 216-226.

695.   O revoliutsionnom dvizhenii na vostoke. [The Revolutionary
Movement in the East.]
Interview given to Mr. Fuse, Japanese correspondent of
Nichi-Nichi. Published in P*, July 4, 1925.
VII, 227-231.

696.   Letter to the Cossacks of Goriachevodskaia stanitsa of Tersk
District, Aug. 18, 1925.
Published in Sovetskii Iug (Rostov-na-Donu), Aug. 25, 192
according to Proletarskaia Revoliutsiia, p. 198. This issue
Sovetskii Iug has been excised from the bound set in the Karl
Marx Library, Rostov-na-Donu.

697.   Letter to Molotov, Sept. 12, 1925.
VII, 375-376 (read by Stalin in the conclusion on the
political report to the Twelfth Party Congress).

698.   Letter to Ermakovskii, Sept. 15, 1925.
Signed, first published in S.
VII, 232-234.

699.   Interview with Participants in Agitprop Conference, Oct. 14,
1925.
First published in S.
VII, 235-240.

700.   Statement to Central Committee, Oct. 19, 1925.
Excerpt in L. Rubinshtein, V bor'be za leninskuiu
natsional'nuiu politiku* (Kazan, Tatizdat, 1930), pp. 100-101

701.   Greeting to Baltic Workers.
Signed, published in I*, Oct. 27, 1925.

702.   Replies to Questions from Komsomolskaia Pravda.
Signed, published in Komsomolskaia Pravda, Oct. 29,
1925.
VII, 245-249.

703.   Letter to Frunze, Oct. 29, 1925.
Signed "Koba," published in S. Borisov, M.V. Frunze*
(Moscow, Voenizdat, 1940), p. 301.

704.   Telegram to Voroshilov, Oct. 31, 1925.
            Attributed to Stalin in P*, Nov. 11, 1925, with quotation
        of whole or excerpt.

705.   Speech at Frunze's funeral, Nov. 3, 1925.
            Published in P*, Nov. 5, 1925.
        VII, 250-251.

706.   Oktiabr', Lenin i perspektivy nashego razvitiia. [October,
        Lenin and the Prospects of Our Development.]
            Signed article in P*, Nov. 7, 1925.
        VII, 252-256.

707.   Letter to the Presidium of the Sokolnichi Party Conference,
        Nov. 18, 1925.
            Signed, published in P*, Nov. 20, 1925.

708.   Letter to the Presidium of the Twenty-Second Leningrad Gu-
        berniia Party Conference, Dec. 8, 1925.
            Signed, published in Krasnaia Letopis'*, no. 1, 1934,
        p. 27.
        VII, 257-258.

709.   Memo to Opposition, Dec. 15, 1925.
            Signed by Kalinin, Stalin, Bukharin, Rykov, Rudzutak,
        Molotov, Dzerzhinskii, read by Stalin in conclusion on
        political report to Fourteenth Party Congress (see entry
        710), published in S, VII, 388-389, omitting the signa-
        tures of Bukharin, Rykov and Rudzutak.

710.   Statements at Fourteenth Party Congress, Dec. 18-31,
        1925.
            Political Report, Dec. 18. Published in P*, Dec. 20, 22,
        1925.
        VII, 261-352.

            Conclusion on Political Report, Dec. 23. Published in P*,
        Dec. 29, 1925; S, p. 365, last line, should read: "etomu my
        stoim i budem stoiat za Bukharina...." P. 384, line 27, after
        "...khotiat ot Bukharina?", the following is omitted from S:

"Oni trebiuiut krovi tov. Bukharina. Imenno etogo trebuet
tov. Zinoviev, zaostriaia vopros v zakliuchitel'nom slove
no Bukharine. Krovi Bukharina trebuete? Ne dadim vam
ego krovi, tak i znaite. (Aplodismenty. Kriki 'pravil'no.'")
VII, 353-391.

Statement in Discussion, Dec. 23. Apparently published
neither in P nor S, but in Chetyrnadtsatyi s"ezd VKP(b).
Stenograficheskii otchet* (Moscow, Gos. izd., 1926), p. 253

1926

711.   O bor'be s pravymi i "ul'tralevymi" uklonami. [The Fight
against Right and "Ultra-Left" Deviations.]
    Two speeches to the Presidium of the Executive Commit-
tee of the Comintern, Jan. 22, 1926, published in P*,
    Feb. 18, 1926.
VIII, 1-10.

712.   Preface to first Edition of Voprosy leninizma, "Jan., 1926."
    Published in collection Voprosy leninizma,* Feb. 1926;
3rd ed., later in 1926, is same as version in S.
VIII, 11-12.

713.   K voprosam leninizma. [Concerning Question of Leninism.]
    Essay signed Jan. 25, 1926. 3rd ed., Moscow, 1926, is
same as S version except for omission of "tovarishch" preceding names of oppositionists in S.
VIII, 13-90.

714.   Letter to Boltnev, Efremov and Ivlev, Feb. 9, 1926.
    Signed, first published in S.
VIII, 91-94.

715.   Letter to Pokoev, Feb. 10, 1926.
    Signed, first published in S.
VIII, 95-98.

716.   Letter to Editor of Bol'shevik, Feb. 17, 1926.
    Signed, published in B*, no. 4, 1926, p. 95.

717.   Eulogy to Kotovskii.
          Signed, published in Kommunist (Kharkov), Feb. 23, 1926.
       VIII, 99.

718.   Speech to French Commission of the Sixth Plenum of the Execu-
       tive Committee of the Comintern, March 6, 1926.
          First published in S.
       VIII, 100-107.

719.   K mezhdunarodnomu kommunisticheskomu zhenskomu dniu.
       [International Communist Women's Day.]
          Signed article in P*, March 7, 1926.
       VIII, 108.

720.   Speech to German Commission of the Sixth Plenum of the Execu-
       tive Committee of the Comintern, March 8, 1926.
          Published in Kommunisticheskii Internatsional*, no. 3,
       1926.
       VIII, 109-115.

721.   Speech to Orgburo, March 5, 1926.
          Published in Izvestiia Tsentral'nogo Komiteta Vsesoiuznoi
       Kommunisticheskoi Partii (b)*, May 3, 1926.

722.   Greeting to Seventh Congress of Komsomol.
          Signed, published in P*, March 23, 1926.

723.   Speech to Central Committee, April, 1926.
          Excerpt published in Biulleten' Oppozitsii*, no. 29-30,
       drawn from original stenogram, p. 110, (same excerpt and
       source citation in Trotsky Archives*, Houghton Library,
       Harvard University, item T 3042).

724.   O khoziaistvennom polozhenii Sovetskogo Soiuza i politike partii.
       [The Economic Situation of the Soviet Union and the Policy of
       the Party.]
          Speech to the activists of the Leningrad party organization,
       April 13, 1926, published in Leningradskaia Pravda, Apr.
       18, 1926.
       VIII, 116-148.

725. Letter to Kaganovich and other Members of Politburo of Ukrainian Party, April 26, 1926.
     Signed, first published in full in S. Published in part in the collection I. Stalin "Marksizm i Natsional'no-kolonial'ny: vopros," Moscow, 1934, pp. 172-173.
     VIII, 149-154.

726. Greeting to Workers of "Zages" (trans. from the Georgia).
     Signed, published in Zaria Vostoka (Tiflis), June 3, 1926, according to Kniga i Proletarskaia Revoliutsiia, p. 148.

727. Bor'ba za pobedu sotsialisticheskogo stroitel'stva. [The Struggle for the Victory of Socialist Construction.]
     Published in Zaria Vostoka (Tiflis), June 3, 1926, according to Kniga i Proletarskaia Revoliutsiia, p. 148.

728. Ob angliiskoi zabastovke i sobytiiakh v Pol'she. [The British Strike and the Events in Poland.]
     Report at a meeting of workers of the Chief Railroad Workshops in Tiflis, June 8, 1926, published in Zaria Vostok (Tiflis), June 10, 1926.
     VIII, 155-172.

729. Reply to Greetings at the Workers of the Chief Railroad Workshops in Tiflis, June 8, 1926.
     Published in Zaria Vostoka (Tiflis), June 10, 1926.
     VIII, 173-175.

730. Greeting to Rabochei Pravde (Tiflis).
     Signed, published in Rabochaia Pravda, July 8, 1926, according to Proletarskaia Revoliutsiia, p. 199.

731. Zigzagi oppozitsii po otnoshenii k Gomindanu. [Zigzags of the Opposition with Respect to the Kuomintang.]
     Speech to the 1st Plenum of the Central Committee and Central Control Commission, during July 14-23, 1926, published in Fakty i tsifry protiv likvidatsii i pererozhdeniia (Leningrad, Priboi, 1927), p. 161, according to Kniga i Proletarskaia Revoliutsiia, p. 148.

732. Ob anglo-russkom komitete edinstva. [The Anglo-Russian Unity Committee.] (abbreviated)
     Speech to 1st Plenum Central Committee and Central Control Commission, July 15, 1926, published in Stalin, Ob oppozitsii* (Moscow, 1928), pp. 295-308.
     VIII, 176-191.

733. Eulogy to Dzerzhinskii, July 22, 1926.
          Signed, published in P*, July 22, 1926.
      VIII, 192-193.

734. Ob anglo-russkom komitete. [The Anglo-Russian Committee.]
          Speech to the Presidium of the Comintern Executive Com-
      mittee, Aug. 7, 1926, first published in S.
      VIII, 194-203.

735. Ob uspekhakh i nedostatkakh kampanii za rezhim ekonomii.
      [Successes and Shortcomings in the Campaign for a Regime
      of Economy.]
          Signed by Stalin, Rykov and Kuibyshev, published in P*,
      Aug. 17, 1926.

736. Letter to the Editor of the "Daily Worker," Sept. 21, 1926.
          Signed, published in Daily Worker* (Chicago), Sept. 30,
      1926.
      VIII, 204-205.

737. Letter to Slepkov, Oct. 8, 1926.
          Signed, first published in S.
      VIII, 206-208.

738. O merakh smiagcheniia vnutripartiinoi bor'by. [Measures for
      Mitigating the Intra-party Struggle.]
          Speech to Politburo, Oct. 11, 1926, first published in S.
      VIII, 209-213.

739. Ob oppozitsionnom bloke v VKP(b). [The Opposition Bloc in the
      CPSU (B).]
          Theses published in P*, Oct. 26, 1926.
      VIII, 214-233.

740. Statements at Fifteenth Party Conference, Oct. 26-Nov. 3, 1926.

          Speech of Nov. 1: O sotsial-demokraticheskom uklone v
      nashei partii (The Social-Democratic Deviation in Our Party)
      VIII, 234-297.

          Conclusion, Nov. 3.
      VIII, 298-356.

The above are published in P*, Nov. 5, 6, and 12, respectively, VIII, 311, last line should read: "Ia dumaiu,
chto prav tut Lenin a ne tov. Riazanov. Ia ochen' uvazhaiu
tov. Riazanova, no dolzhen priznat'sia chto eschche bol'she
uvazhal i prodolzhaiu uvazhat' tov. Lenina. "

741. O perspektivakh revoliutsii v Kitae. [The Prospects of the
Revolution in China.]
      Speech to the Chinese Commission of the Comintern Exec
tive Committee, [7th Plenum], Nov. 30, 1926, published in
Kommunisticheskii Internatsional*, Dec. 10, pp. 357-374.
"Primechanie, " in S, VIII, 373, did not appear in the ori-
ginal published version.
VIII, 357-374.

742. Statements at Seventh Enlarged Plenum of Executive Committee
of Comintern, Nov. 22 - Dec. 16, 1926.

      Speech of Dec. 7. Eshche raz o sotsial-demokraticheskon
uklone v nashei partii. [Once More on the Social-Democratic
Deviation in Our Party.]
IX, 3-61.

      Conclusion, Dec. 13. Published in P*, Dec. 19, 21, 22, 192
IX, 62-151.

      Statement of Dec. 15. Only in Puti mirovoi revoliutsii.
VII Rasshirennyi plenum IKKI* (Moscow, Gosizdat, 1927),
vol. II, pp. 342-343.

743. Letter to Ksenofontov, Dec. 30, 1926.
      First published in S.
IX, 152-154.

1927

744. Speech to 15th Moscow Guberniia Party Conference, Jan. 14, 1
      Published in P*, Jan. 16, 1928.
IX, 155-162.

745. Letter to Zaitsev, Jan. 28, 1927.
      Signed, first published in S.
IX, 163-166.

746.   Greeting to the Lena Workers, Feb. 22, 1927.
          Signed, published in <u>Lenskii Shakhter</u>, April 17, 1927.
    IX, 167-168.

747.   Greeting to <u>Bor'ba</u> (Stalingrad), Feb. 22, 1927.
          Signed, published in <u>Bor'ba</u>, May 31, 1927.
    IX, 169.

748.   Speech at Stalin Railroad Shops, October Railroad, March 1, 1927.
          Abbreviated version in <u>P</u>*, March 3, 1927.
    IX, 170-175.

749.   Letter to Svetkov and Alypov, March 7, 1927.
          Signed, first published in <u>S</u>.
    IX, 176-178.

750.   Letter to Dmitriev, undated.
          Published in <u>B</u>*, no. 6, 1927.
    IX, 179-190.

751.   Letter to Shinkevich, March 20, 1927.
          Signed, first published in <u>S</u>.
    IX, 191-192.

752.   Speech to Fifth Komsomol Conference, March 29, 1927.
          Published in <u>P</u>*, March 31, 1927.
    IX, 193-202.

753.   Speech to Moscow Party Workers, April 6, 1927.
          Vuyo Vuyovitch, addressing the Eighth Plenum of the
E.C.C.I. in May, 1927, claimed to produce a transcript of
this speech made by himself on April 6, 1927, and in defense
of its accuracy notes that he was once a Comintern congress
translator. An English translation of this version of Stalin's
presumed speech appears in Trotsky, <u>Problems of the</u>
<u>Chinese Revolution</u>* (New York: Pioneer Press, 1932), pp.
389-390. It does not appear that this purports to be the entire
original speech in translation, although lack of clear editorial
form makes this unclear.

754.   Letter to Chugunov, April 9, 1927.
             Signed, first published in S.
         IX, 203-204.

755.   Letter to Ian--skii, undated.
             Signed, published in B*, no. 7, 1927, pp. 127-135.
         IX, 205-220.

756.   Voprosy kitaiskoi revoliutsii. [Questions of the Chinese Revo-
         lution.]
             Unsigned theses published in P*, April 21, 1927. P. 222,
         line 6, "postepenno" added in S. P. 223, line 12, "inostranny
         omitted after "obrazom." P. 227, line 3, "politicheskoi"
         added in S.
         IX, 221-230.

757.   Greeting to Pravda.
             Signed, published in P*, May 5, 1927.
         IX, 231.

758.   K voprosam kitaiskoi revoliutsii. [Concerning Questions of the
         Chinese Revolution.]
             Letter to Marchulin, signed May 9, 1927, published in
         Derevenskii Kommunist, May 15, 1927.
         IX, 232-238.

759.   Interview with Students at Sun Yat-Sen University, May 13, 1927.
             Published in Stalin, Revoliutsiia v Kitae i oshibki oppo-
         zitsii* (Moscow, Gos. 12d., 1927), pp. 5-31.
         IX, 239-268.

760.   O lozunge diktatury proletariata i bedneishego krest'ianstva v
         period podgotovki Oktiabria. [The Slogan of the Dictatorship of
         the Proletariat in the Period of the Preparation for October.]
             Letter to S. Pokrovskii, May 20, 1927, published without
         signature in Voprosy leninizma*, 4th edition, 1928.
         IX, 269-281.

761.   Revoliutsiia v Kitae i zadachi kominterna. [The Revolution in
         China and the Tasks of the Comintern.]

Speech to the Comintern Executive Committee (8th Plenum), May 24, 1927, published in B*, no. 10, 1927.
IX, 282-312.

762.   Greeting to Students of Communist University of Toilers of the East.
Signed, published in P*, May 31, 1927.
IX, 313-314.

763.   Letter to Chinese Communists, June 1, 1927.
According to H. Isaacs, The Tragedy of the Chinese Revolution (Stanford, Stanford University Press, 1951), pp. 245-246, this letter is by Stalin. It is given in nearly complete form in the course of Stalin's speech of Aug. 1 to the Central Committee and Central Control Commission (X, 32-33). However, in this context Stalin treats the document as if it were not his own work, even though he approves of the context.

764.   Letter to S. Pokrovsky, June 23, 1927.
Signed, first published in S.
IX, 315-321.

765.   Letter to the Editor of The Daily Worker.
Signed, published in The Daily Worker*, July 27, 1927.

766.   Zametki na sovremennye temy. [Notes on Contemporary Themes.]
Signed article in P*, July 28, 1927.
IX, 322-361.

767.   Statements at 1st Plenum of Central Committee and Central Control Commission, July 29-Aug. 9, 1927.

Speech of Aug. 1.
X, 3-59.

Speech of Aug. 5.
X, 60-84.

Speech of Aug. 9.
X, 85-91.

All of above were first published in Stalin, Ob oppozitsii*
(Moscow, Gosizdat, 1928). P. 37, line 19, should read
"...bor'by za razlozhenie i..."

P. 38, line 20, should read "...chtoby dvinut' shchupal'ts
v eti..."

P. 41, line 8, should read "...svobodu kritiki, svobodu
politvat' pochem zria reiaktsionnykh liderov..."

P. 43, line 26, "naklevetali" should read "nabrekhali."

P. 51, lines 10 and 11, "revoliutsionnoe dvizhenie" should
read "revoliutsiia."

768.　Interview with American Workers' Delegation, Sept. 9, 1927.
　　　Published in P*, Sept. 15, 1927. P. 135, line 18, should
　　　conclude: "Ibo okonchatel'noe porazhenie mirovogo kapitaliz-
　　　ma est' pobeda sotsializma na arene mirovogo khoziaistva."
　　　X, 92-148.

769.　Letter to M.I. Ulianova, Sept. 16, 1927. (Reply to L. Mikhelson
　　　Signed, first published in S.
　　　X, 149-152.

770.　Politicheskaia fizionomiia russkoi oppozitsii. [The Political
　　　Complexion of the Russian Opposition.]
　　　Speech to the Comintern Executive Committee and Inter-
　　　national Control Commission, Sept. 27, 1927, published in
　　　Kommunisti cheskii International*, Oct. 14, 1927. (Excerpt)

771.　Konspekt stat'i "Mezhdunarodnyi kharakter Oktiabr'skoi Revo-
　　　liutsii." [Synopsis of the article "The International Character
　　　of the October Revolution."]
　　　Signed October, 1927; previously unpublished in this pre-
　　　liminary form; the article itself was published Nov. 6, 7,
　　　1927 (X, 168-171).
　　　X, 168-171.

772.   Statement at Central Committee, Oct. 1927.
        Ruth Fischer, Stalin and German Communism (Cambridge,
        Harvard University Press, 1948), p. 593, provides excerpt
        drawn from Die Fahne des Kommunismus, Nov. 18, 1927.

773.   Trotskistskaia oppozitsiia prezhde i teper'. [The Trotskyist
        Opposition Before and Now.]
        Speech to the Central Committee and Central Control Com-
        mission, Oct. 23, 1929, published in P*, Nov. 2, 1927. P.
        175, line 24, omits the following after "Eto sovershenno
        verno": "Davaite prochtem eto mesto, khotia ono i chitalos'
        ran'shev plenume neskol'ko raz. Vot ono, 'Stalin slishkom
        grub, i etot nedostatiiok vpolne terpimyi v srede i v obsh-
        chenii mezhdu nami, kommunistami, stanovitsia neterpimym
        v dolzhnosti genseka. Poetomu ia predlagaiu tovarishcham
        obdumat' sposob peremeshcheniia Stalina s etogo mesta i
        naznachit' na eto mesto drugogo cheloveka, kotoryi vo vsekh
        drugikh otnosheniiakh otlichaetsia ot tov. Stalina tol'ko odnim
        perevesom, imenno bolee terpim, bolee loialen, bolee
        vezhliv i bolee vnimatelen k tovarishcham, men'she kapriz-
        nosti, i t. d." Stalin is quoting from Lenin's "Testament."
        X, 172-205.

774.   Interview with Foreign Workers' Delegations, Nov. 5, 1927.
        Published in P*, Nov. 13, 15, 1927. P. 207, line 18,
        "pri nyneshnikh usloviakh" added in S.
        X, 206-238.

775.   Mezhdunarodnyi kharakter Oktiabr'skoi Revoliutsii. [The Inter-
        national Character of the October Revolution.]
        Signed article in P*, Nov. 6, 7, 1927.
        X, 239-250.

776.   Greeting to Party Conference of Moscow Military District.
        Signed, published in Krasnaia Zvezda, Nov. 18, 1927.
        X, 251.

777.   Partiia i oppozitsiia. [The Party and the Opposition.]
        Speech to party conference of Moscow gubernia, Nov. 23,
        1927, published in P*, Nov. 24, 1927.
        X, 252-268.

778.   Statements at Fifteenth Party Congress, Dec. 2-19, 1927.

Political Report, Dec. 3. Published in P*, Dec. 6, 1927.
P. 283, line 28, "na stadiiu organizatsii sovetov" should
follow "stadiiu"; p. 287, line 23, "priznanie Uragvaem"
should follow "kreditakh."
X, 271-353.

Conclusion on Political Report, Dec. 7. Published in P*,
Dec. 9, 1927.
X, 354-371.

779.   Statement to Foreign Press Represenatives, Dec. 16, 1927.
Signed, published in P*, Dec. 18, 1927.
X, 372-375.

1928

780.   Speeches in Siberia, Jan., 1928.
Evidently a composite speech made up of excerpts from
various statements, first published in S.
XI, 1-9.

781.   Greeting to G.I. Petrovskii.
Signed, published in P*, Feb. 7, 1928.

782.   Pervye itogi zagotovitel'noi kampanii i dalneishie zadachi partii.
[First Results of the Procurement Campaign and the Further
Tasks of the Party.]
Announcement, Feb. 13, 1928, signed, first published in S
XI, 10-19.

783.   Greeting to Red Army.
Signed, published in Krasnaia Zvezda, Feb. 23, 1928.
XI, 20.

784.   O trekh osobennostiakh Krasnoi Armii. [Three Distinctive
Features of the Red Army.]
Speech to the Moscow Soviet, Feb. 25, 1928, published
in P*, Feb. 28, 1928.
XI, 21-26.

785.   O rabotakh aprel'skogo ob''edinennogo plenuma TsK i TsKK.
        [The Work of the April Joint Penum of the Central Committee
        and Central Control Commission.]
            Speech to the activists of the Moscow party organization,
        April 13, 1928, published in P*, April 18, 1928. The last
        22 lines on p. 55 did not appear in P; according to an edi-
        torial note on p. 27, these were part of the original record
        and were "restored" in S. Also, on p. 55, line 6, "osvobo-
        ditel'nuiu" appears in S in place of "revoliutsionnomu," and
        on lines 7-8 "kapitalisty Evropy i Ameriki" appears in place
        of "zapadno-evropeiskie burzhua."
        XI, 27-64.

786.   Greeting to Workers of Kostroma, April 30, 1928.
            Signed, published in Severnaia Pravda, May 4, 1928.
        XI, 65.

787.   Speech to the Eighth Congress of the Komsomol, May 16, 1928.
            Published in P*, May 17, 1928.
        XI, 66-77.

788.   Greeting to Komsomolskaia Pravda, May 26, 1928.
            Signed, published in Komsomolskaia Pravda, May 27, 1928.
        XI, 78-79.

789.   Greeting to Sverdlov University.
            Signed, published in P*, May 27, 1928.
        XI, 80.

790.   Na khlebnom fronte. [On the Grain Front.]
            Speech to the Institute of Red Professors, Communist
        Academy and Sverdlov University, May 28, 1928, published
        in P*, June 2, 1928.
        XI, 81-97.

791.   Letter to Members of the Party Affairs Study Circle of the
        Communist Academy, June 8, 1928.
            Signed, published in Komsomol'skaia Pravda, April 19,
            1928.
        XI, 98-100.

792.   Letter to S., June 12, 1928.
           Signed, published in P*, July 3, 1928. Editorial note,
        p. 101, says published version is slightly abridged.
        XI, 101-115.

793.   Letter to the Politburo, June 20, 1928. (Reply to Fromkin)
           Signed, first published in S.
        XI, 116-126.

794.   Protiv oposhleniia lozunga samokritiki. [Against Vulgarizing
        the Slogan of Self-Criticism.]
           Signed article in P*, June 26, 1928.
        XI, 127-138.

795.   Statements in Central Committee Meeting, July 4-12, 1928.

           Speech of July 5.
        XI, 141-156.

           Speech of July 9.
        XI, 157-187.

           Speech of July 11.
        XI, 188-196.

        All of above first published in S.

796.   Ob itogakh iiul'skogo plenuma TsK VKP (b). [Results of the
        July Plenum of the CC of the ACP(b).]
           Speech to the activists of the Leningrad party organization
        July 13, 1928, published in Leningradskaia Pravda, July 14,
        1928.
        XI, 197-218.

797.   Greeting to the Leningrad Proletariat.
           Signed, published in Krasnaia Gazeta, July 15, 1928,
        according to Proletarskaia Revoliutsiia, p. 202.

798.   Greeting to the Leningrad Osoviakhim.
           Signed, published in Krasnaia Zvezda, July 15, 1928.
        XI, 219.

799. Letter to Kuibyshev, Aug. 31, 1928.
            Signed, first published in S.
      XI, 220.

800. Eulogy for Skvortsova-Stepanova.
            Signed, published in P*, Oct. 9, 1928.
      XI, 221.

801. O pravoi opasnosti v VKP(b). [The Right Danger in the ACP
      (b).]
            Speech to the Plenum of the Moscow Party Committee and
      Control Commission, Oct. 19, 1928, published in P*, Oct.
      23, 1928.
      XI, 222-238.

802. Letter to Shu--u, Oct. 27, 1928.
            Signed, first published in S.
      XI, 239-241.

803. Greeting to Komsomol.
            Signed, published in P*, Oct. 28, 1928.
      XI, 242-243.

804. Greeting to Working Women and Peasant Women.
            Signed, published in P*, Nov. 17, 1928.
      XI, 244.

805. Ob industrializatsii strany i o pravom uklone v VKP(b). [In-
      dustrialization of the Country and the Right Deviation in the
      ACP(b).]
            Speech to the Central Committee, Nov. 19, 1928, pub-
      lished in P*, Nov. 24, 1928.
      XI, 245-290.

806. Congratulations to Workers of "Katushka" Factory, Iartsevo
      Factory of Smolensk Guberniia.
            Signed, published in P*, Nov. 25, 1928.
      IX, 291.

807.	Greeting to the "Red Profintern" Factory, Bezhitsa, Nov. 29, 1⁹
		Signed, published in P*, Nov. 30, 1928.
	XI, 292.

808.	Greeting to Frunze Military Academy.
		Signed, published in P*, Dec. 9, 1928.
	XI, 293.

809.	O pravoi opasnosti v germanskoi kompartii. [The Right Danger
	in the German Communist Party.]
		Speech to the Comintern Executive Committee Presidium,
		Dec. 19, 1928, published in B*, no. 23-24, 1928.
	XI, 294-310.

810.	Letter to Kushtysev, Dec. 28, 1928.
		Signed, first published in S.
	XI, 311-312.

811.	Dokatilis'. [They Have Sunk to the Depths.]
		Article, evidently written between Dec. 28 and 31 but for
		no visible reason, unpublished before S.
	XI, 313-317.

812.	Letter to Eugene Lyons, undated.
		English translation published in E. Lyons, Assignment in
		Utopia (New York, Harcourt, Brace, 1927), pp. 264-265.

813.	Interview with Finskii Vestnik, Dec., 1928.
		Finskii Vestnik, Dec. 17, 1928, according to Francis B.
		Randall, Stalin's Russia. An Historical Reconsideration.
		New York, The Free Press, 1965, pp. 297-298.

1929

814.	Gruppa Bukharina i pravyi uklon v nashei partii'. [Bukharin's
	Group and the Right Deviation in Our Party.]
		Abridged and edited composite of various statements in
		meeting of the Politburo and Presidium of the Central Control

Commission which took place in late January and early February, 1929.
XI, 318-325.

815.   Letter to Bill'-Belotserkovskii, Feb. 2, 1929.
           Signed, first published in S.
       XI, 326-329.

816.   Greeting to Workers of the "Red Triangle" Factory, Feb. 2, 1929.
           Signed, published in Leningradskaia Pravda, Feb. 3, 1929.
       XI, 330.

817.   Greeting to the Proskurov Red Cossack Regiment. Feb. 22, 1929.
           Signed, first published in S.
       XI, 331.

818.   Greeting to Sel'skokhoziaistvennaia Gazeta.
           Signed, published in Sel'skokhoziaistvennaia Gazeta, March 1, 1929.
       XI, 332.

819.   Natsional'nyi vopros i leninizm. [The National Question and Leninism.]
           First published in S, which asserts that it was originally a letter of March 18, 1929, to Meshkov, Kovalchuk and "others."
       XI, 333-355.

820.   O pravom uklone v VKP(b). [The Right Deviation in the ACP(b).]
           Speech to Plenum of Central Committee and Central Control Commission, April 22, 1929. Portions previously published in B*, no. 23-24, 1929, pp. 15-49. S, XII, pp. 1-9, 49-56, 92-95, 96-103, 106-107 published in S for the first time (see XII, 1, fn.), A. Avtorkhanov, Stalin and the Soviet Communist Party (New York, Praeger, 1959), p. 129, claims to have seen a confidential, unpublished stenographic version of the speech and states that the version in S is "mutilated."
       XII, 1-107.

821.   O pravykh fraktsionerakh v amerikanskoi kompartii. [The Right
        Factionalists in the American Communist Party.]
            Three speeches, dated May 6 (to the American commis-
        sion of the Comintern) and May 14 (to the presidium of the
        Comintern Executive Committee--two speeches), 1929, pub-
        lished in B*, no. 1, 1930, pp. 8-26.

822.   Foreword dated May 11, 1929, to Booklet "Sorevnovanie mass"
        by E. Mikulina.
            Also published as signed article in P*, May 22, 1929.
        XII, 108-111.

823.   Letter to F. Kon, July 9, 1929.
            Signed, first published in S.
        XII, 112-115.

824.   Greeting to Ukrainian Komsomol, July 10, 1929.
            Signed, published in P*, July 12, 1929.
        XII, 116.

825.   Entry in Log of "Chervona Ukraina," July 25, 1929.
            First published in Krasnyi Chernomorets (Sevastopol),
        Nov. 7, 1929.
        XII, 117.

826.   God velikogo pereloma. [A Year of Great Change.]
            Signed article, dated Nov. 3, 1929, in P*, Nov. 7, 1929.
        XII, 118-135.

827.   Greeting to Special Far Eastern Army. Oct. 30, 1929.
            Published in P*, Nov. 7, 1929.
        XII, 136.

828.   Neobkhodimaia popravka. [A Necessary Correction.]
            Signed note published in P*, Dec. 18, 1929.
        XII, 137-139.

829.   Statement of Thanks to All Who Sent Stalin Greetings on His
        Fiftieth Birthday, Dec. 21, 1929.
            Signed, published in P*, Dec. 22, 1929.
        XII, 140.

830.   K voprosam agrarnoi politiki v SSSR. [Concerning Questions of
        Agrarian Policy in the USSR.]
            Speech to conference of "Marxist Students of the Agrarian
        Question," Dec. 27, 1929, published in P*, Dec. 29, 1929.
        P. 150, line 26, following "tem samym perekhod" and pre-
        ceding "ot melkogo krest'ianskogo khoziaistva..." the follow-
        ing should appear: "na rel'sy kollektivizma."
        XII, 141-172.

                            1930

831.   Greeting to Stalingrad Workers.
            Signed, published in P*, Jan. 2, 1930.

832.   Letter to Gorky, Jan. 17, 1930.
            Signed, first published in S.
        XII, 173-177.

833.   K voprosu o politike likvidatsii kulachestva, kak klassa. [Con-
        cerning the Policy of Liquidating the Kulaks as a Class.]
            Signed article, dated Jan. 19, 1930, in Krasnaia Zvezda,
        Jan. 21, 1930.
        XII, 178-183.

834.   Reply to Students of Sverdlov University, Feb. 9, 1930.
            Signed, published in P*, Feb. 10, 1930.
        XII, 184-190.

835.   Greeting to the First Cavalry Army.
            Signed, published in P*, Feb. 23, 1930.

836.   Greeting to the Workers of the Izhevsk Factory.
            Signed, published in Izhevskaia Pravda, March 2, 1930,
        according to Proletarskaia Revoliutsiia, p. 203.

837.   Golovokruzhenie ot uspekhov. [Dizzy with Success.]
       Signed article in P*, March 2, 1930.
XII, 191-199.

838.   Letter to Bezymenskii, March 19, 1930.
       Signed, first published in S.
XII, 200-201.

839.   Otvet tovarishcham kolkhoznikam. [Reply to Collective-Farm
Comrades.]
       Signed article in P*, April 3, 1930.
XII, 202-228.

840.   Greeting to "Peninsular Giant" Factory.
       Signed, published in P*, April 24, 1930.

841.   Greeting to the First Graduates of the Industrial Academy,
April 25, 1930.
       Signed, published in P*, April 26, 1930.
XII, 229-230.

842.   Greeting to Shatov.
       Signed, published in P*, April 26, 1930.

843.   Letter to Rafail, May 31, 1930.
       Signed, first published in S.
XII, 231-232.

844.   Greeting to the Agricultural Machinery Factory, Rostov-na-Donu
June 16, 1930.
       Signed, published in P*, June 17, 1930.
XII, 233.

845.   Greeting to the Stalingrad Tractor Factory, June 17, 1930.
       Signed, published in P*, June 18, 1930.
XII, 234.

846.   Statements at Sixteenth Party Congress, June 26--July 13, 1930.

Political Report, June 27.
XII, 235-373.

Conclusion on Political Report, July 2.
XIII, 1-16.

Published in P*, June 29 and July 3, respectively.

847.   Greeting to Kanevsk Kolkhoz.
Signed, published in P*, June 19, 1930.

848.   Letter to Shatunovskii, "August, 1930."
Signed, first published in S.
XIII, 17-19.

849.   Letter to Ch., "November, 1930" (with supplementary note dated Dec. 7, 1930).
Signed, first published in S.
XIII, 20-22.

850.   Letter to Demian Bedny, Dec. 12, 1930.
Excerpts, signed, first published in S.
XIII, 23-27.

1931

851.   Statement to Jewish News Agency of the U.S., Jan. 12, 1931.
Signed, published in P*, Nov. 30, 1936.
XIII, 28.

852.   O zadachakh khoziaistvennikov. [The Tasks of Economic Administrators.]
Speech to the First All-Union Conference of Leading Personnel of Socialist Industry, Feb. 4, 1931, published in P*, Feb. 5, 1931.
XIII, 29-42.

853.   Letter to Etchin, Feb. 27, 1931.
            Signed, first published in S̲.
        XIII, 43-44.

854.   Greeting to Workers of Azneft and Grozneft, March 31, 1931.
            Signed, published in P̲*, April 1, 1931.
        XII, 45.

855.   Greeting to Elektrozavod.
            Signed, published in P̲*, April 3, 1931.
        XIII, 46.

856.   Greeting to Magnitogorsk Workers.
            Signed, published in P̲*, May 19, 1931.
        XIII, 47.

857.   Greeting to MTS Workers.
            Signed, published in P̲*, May 28, 1931.
        XIII, 48-49.

858.   Greeting to the Chairman of the Grain Trust Board.
            Signed, published in P̲*, May 30, 1931. In the original the
        addressee was specifically noted as "T. Gerchikov."
        XIII, 50.

859.   Novaia obstanovka--novye zadachi khoziaistvennogo stroitel'stva
        [New Conditions--New Tasks in Economic Construction.]
            Speech to Conference of Economic Administrators, June 2
        1931, published in P̲*, July 5, 1930.
        XIII, 51-80.

860.   Greeting to Moscow Auto Factory.
            Signed, published in P̲*, Oct. 1, 1931.
        XIII, 81.

861.   Greeting to Kharkov Tractor Factory.
            Signed, published in P̲*, Oct. 1, 1931.
        XIII, 82.

862. Greeting to Newspaper Tekhnika.
    Signed, published in P*, Oct. 10, 1931.
    XIII, 83.

863. Comment on Gorky's story "Devushka i smert'," Oct. 11,
    1931.
    Komsomol'skaia Pravda, Oct. 20, 1937. Short inscription
    in Stalin's hand on Gorky's copy of his story "Smert' i
    devushka." Facsimile of the inscription in Robert Payne,
    The Rise and Fall of Stalin. New York, Simon and Shuster,
    1965, p. 402.

864. Letter to Editorial Board of Proletarskaia Revoliutsiia, "end
    of October," 1931.
    Signed, published in Proletarskaia Revoliutsiia*, no. 6,
    1931, pp. 3-12.
    XIII, 84-102.

865. Greeting to Nizhnii-Novgorod Auto Factory. Nov. 3, 1931.
    Signed by Stalin and Molotov, published in P*, Nov. 4,
    1931.
    XIII, 103.

866. Interview with Emil Ludwig, Dec. 13, 1931.
    Published in B*, no. 8, 1932.
    XIII, 104-123.

1932

867. Greeting to Director of Nizhnii-Novgorod Auto Factory.
    Signed, published in P*, Jan. 2, 1932.
    XIII, 124.

868. Letter to Directors of Saratov Combine Project and Combine
    Works, Jan. 4, 1932.
    Signed, published in P*, Jan. 5, 1932.
    XIII, 125.

869.   Letter to Olekhnovich, Jan. 15, 1932.
             Signed, published in B*, no. 16, 1932.
         XIII, 126-130.

870.   Letter to Aristov, Jan. 25, 1932.
             Signed, published in B*, no. 16, 1932.
         XIII, 130-132.

871.   Greeting to Magnitostroi. Mar. 29, 1932.
             Signed, published in P*, March 30, 1932.
         XIII, 133.

872.   Letter to Richardson.
             Signed, published in P*, April 3, 1932.
         XIII, 134.

873.   O znachehii i zadachakh biuro zhalob. [The Importance and
         Tasks of the Complaints Bureau.]
             Signed article in P*, April 7, 1932.
         XIII, 135-136.

874.   Replies to Ralph Barnes, May 3, 1932.
             First published in S.
         XIII, 137-139.

875.   Greeting to Kuznetskstroi.
             Signed, published in P*, May 24, 1932.
         XIII, 140.

876.   Greeting to Seventh Conference of Komsomol, July 8, 1932.
             Signed, published in P*, July 9, 1932.
         XIII, 141.

877.   Greeting to Gorky.
             Signed, published in P*, Sept. 25, 1932.
         XIII, 142.

878.   Greeting to Dnieprostroi.
           Signed, published in P*, Oct. 10, 1932.
       XIII, 143.

879.   Greeting to Leningrad.
           Signed, published in P*, Nov. 7, 1932.
       XIII, 144.

880.   Letter to Pravda.
           Signed, published in P*, Nov. 18, 1932.
       XIII, 145.

881.   Speech to Politburo and Presidium of Control Commission,
       Nov. 27, 1932.
           Excerpts published in B*, no. 1-2, 1933.

882.   Greeting to OGPU.
           Signed, published in P*, Dec. 20, 1932.
       XIII, 158.

883.   Gospodin Kempbell priviraet. [Mr. Campbell Stretches the
       Truth.]
           Signed, dated Dec. 23, 1932, published in B*, no. 22,
           1932, giving the date as Dec. 23, 1932 and which seems to
           be the correct date. Includes interview with Campbell on
           Jan. 28, 1928.
       XIII, 146-157.

                            1933

884.   Statements at 1st Plenum of Central Committee and Central
       Control Commission, Jan. 7-12, 1933.

           Speech of Jan. 7.
       XIII, 161-215.

           Speech of Jan. 11.
       XIII, 216-233.

           Published in P*, Jan. 10 and 17, respectively.

885.   Greeting to Rabotnitsa.
            Signed, published in P*, Jan. 26, 1933.
        XIII, 234.

886.   Letter to I. N. Bazhanov, Feb. 16, 1933.
            Signed, first published in S.
        XIII, 235.

887.   Speech to First All-Union Congress of Collective Farm Shock
       Brigaders, Feb. 19, 1933.
            Published in P*, Feb. 23, 1933.
        XIII, 236-256.

888.   Greeting to Red Army.
            Signed, published in P*, Feb. 23, 1933.
        XIII, 257.

889.   Letter to Ralph Barnes, March 20, 1933.
            Signed, first published in S.
        XIII, 258.

889a. Letter to M. A. Sholokhov.
            Quoted at length by Khrushchev, who states that it is a
        reply to a letter from Sholokhov dated Apr. 16, 1933 (date of
        reply not given), in O Kommunisticheskom vospitanii (Mosco
        Izd. Polit. Lit., 1964), p. 224. Khrushchev revealed the
        letter in a speech of Mar. 8, 1963.

890.   Letter to Budennyi.
            Signed, published in P*, April 26, 1933.
        XIII, 259.

891.   Interview with Col. Robins, May 13, 1933.
            First published in S. "Brief record."
        XIII, 260-273.

892.   Greeting to Komsomol, Oct. 28, 1933.
            Signed, published in P*, Oct. 29, 1933.
        XIII, 274-275.

893.   Interview with W. Duranty, Dec. 25, 1933.
            Published in P*, Jan. 4, 1934.
        XIII, 276-281.

1934

894.   Statements at Seventeenth Party Congress, Jan. 26-Feb. 10,
       1934.

              Report of Jan. 26.
       XIII, 282-379.

              Conclusion of Political Report, Jan. 31.
       XIII, 381.

              Published in P*, Jan. 28 and Feb. 1, 1934, respectively.

895.   Greeting to Frunze Military Academy.
              Signed, published in P*, Jan. 18, 1934.
       XIII, 380.

PART TWO

1934 - 1953

PART II

INTRODUCTION

The opening of the year 1934 has often been regarded as a major juncture in the history of Russian communism,[1] and it is ironic
that Stalin should have died just at the time when the serial publication
of the volumes of his Sochineniia had reached this point in their coverage, ceasing there because of the reticence of his successors to con-
tinue the "cult of personality" in full flower. As a result of this coinci-
dence, those interested in Stalin's writings have the assistance of the
official anthology--whatever its drawbacks--just up to the point when
mature Stalinist totalitarianism is often considered to have started, but
lack a comparable guide to the years of his life in which his power was
at its zenith.

One might think that the task of collecting the public papers of
a dictator from the years of his dominance would be a more substantial
task than that of gathering up his earlier works. Certainly this is the
case with Khrushchev, whose publications before 1953 and even before
1957 are slender, compared to the mass of printed verbiage attributed
to him in the years 1957-64. But Stalin's attainment of unchallenged
supremacy led to a remarkably sharp curtailment of public statements
(excepting republication of older "classics," of course). The demigod

---

[1] This was reflected in the spirit of the Fourteenth Party Congress of January 1934, "the congress of the victors." The last item
in the published volumes of Stalin's Sochineniia is his address to this
body. The distinguished historian of the CPSU in its later years, John
Armstrong, has chosen this point as the beginning of his work The
Politics of Totalitarianism (New York, Random House, 1961). See also
Istoriia VKP (b). Kratkii Kurs for emphasis on this juncture.

149

who was so ubiquitous in Soviet Russia chose to ration out his wisdom with a parsimony seemingly based on a shrewd desire to avoid the disease of modern communications sometimes known as overexposure. Thus it is that speeches and other papers attributed to Stalin in the years of his greatest importance, the years following the period covered in the thirteen volumes of the Sochineniia, are relatively sparse and pose bibliographical problems largely unlike those raised by the earlier material.

For one thing, there is very little need to search for published materials appearing in fairly obscure books and serials. In keeping with the exalted status of the Leader after 1934, the editors of Pravda saw to it that nearly everything that was released for publication over Stalin's name appeared in that newspaper, generally on the front page. True, Stalin somewhat whimsically had certain materials published in the theoretical bimonthly Bol'shevik instead of Pravda, but between these two obvious periodicals one can find all the works published by Stalin from 1934 to 1953 with only insignificant exceptions.[2] This observation is confirmed not only by my searches of various Soviet publications that might have carried Stalin material, but also by the more comprehensive efforts of Soviet bibliographers. One has not only the several bibliographies covering the period to 1939, noted in the Introduction to Part I of the present bibliography, but also the work of a team that devoted its efforts to the wartime years.[3] The problem--and the objective of the bibliographer--is not so much to locate all the published

---

[2]Therefore, no asterisks will be used to show which works have been successfully tracked to their earliest published version--all were.

[3]Publichnaia Biblioteka imeni V.I. Lenina, "Vystupleniia, prikazy, privetstviia tovarishcha I.V. Stalina za gody Velikoi Otchestvennoi Voiny 1941-1945. Bibliograficheskii ukazatel'" (Moscow, 1945, 143 pp.)

items bearing Stalin's name as it is to determine which items are really his work in any meaningful sense and which merit inclusion in a bibliography designed to assist scholars--not to inundate them with references that would only confuse the picture. This problem cannot be adequately treated by an attempt to distinguish between Stalin's own handiwork and that of ghost-writers or secretaries. At least as early as his major addresses of the later twenties Stalin must have been utilizing speech-writers of some sort in the manner of almost all states-men of this century. But it is quite clear that even the longest official reports not only reflect Stalin's policies but also bear the distinct im-press of his mode of thought and style of expression. That his longer and more laborious writings should not be dismissed as his assistants' work is suggested by the Khrushchevian treatment of the famous essay "O dialekticheskom i istoricheskom materializme" and the book in which it appeared as a chapter, the equally famous Istoriia VKP(b). Kratkii kurs. The essay is long and weighty (at least, leaden) enough to suggest that no busy politician would have written it without a good deal of help. Nevertheless, this writing was attributed to Stalin per-sonally in his own time and afterwards. The history book as a whole was from 1946 to 1956 attributed directly to Stalin's pen, but in 1956 Khrushchev explicitly stated that the larger work was composed by a committee. The implication is that the amount of ghosting that went into the essay on materialism was not so great as to deprive Stalin of credit as the author, whereas the history book was so much the work of specialists that Stalin should not be given credit for it, even though this particular work is Stalinist in the extreme and represents his point of view as directly as many ghost-written works represent their alleged authors. The scholar therefore seems justified in treating a number of longer works bearing Stalin's name as his own, despite the indetermi-nate role of secretarial assistance. This conclusion, does not, however, cover the cases in which published writings do not bear Stalin's name

as author, but seem likely to have been more or less dictated or edited
by him. For example, Khrushchev has stated that Stalin personally revised the manuscript of his short biography, making parts of it as much
his own work as many ghost-written documents are the work of their
alleged authors. Moreover, the published letters to the Yugoslav Communist Party are a good example of state papers of such critical importance that one assumes Stalin had a direct hand in their preparation;
indeed, Hoxha of Albania has alluded to the letters as if they were
pretty nearly Stalin's work.[4] But the difficulty in selecting Stalinist
works that might well be treated as Stalin's works is in knowing when
to stop. Owing to the remarkable extent of his control over his lieutenants and all media of communication during the years of unchallenged
supremacy, it is practically impossible to know where to draw the line
between "Stalinist" and "Stalin's." I have taken the simple but not
wholly satisfactory course of omitting documents not actually signed by
Stalin in their original published form.

But it would be self-defeating for a bibliographer to list all the
materials bearing Stalin's signature and published after early 1934.
For although the assistance of secretaries in the preparation of the
larger works does not seem to have de-Stalinized their essence, there
is a large body of material which bears Stalin's name but is in essence
the work of staff assistants assigned to certain routine activities. During the war years, for example, a great many senior military promotions
were officially announced in Pravda over the signatures of Stalin and Ia.
Chadaev, who signed for records administration of the Sovnarkom.[5]
Especially toward the end of the war Pravda carried a large number of

---

[4]E. Hoxha speech of Nov. 7, 1961, in Zeri i Popullit, Nov. 8,
1961, according to A. Dallin et al. (eds.), Diversity in International
Communism. A Documentary Record, 1961-1963 (New York, Columbia
University Press, 1963), p. 112. Here Hoxha even refers to Stalin and
Molotov as signatories.

[5]E.G., Pravda, February 18, 1945.

very brief notes of thanks signed by Stalin and addressed to various factories, kolhozy, and the like for having donated a sum of money to the war effort.[6] Also in the war years, and more so after the victory of the U.S.S.R., one also finds large clusters of short notes of thanks to various foreign (mostly non-Communist) statesmen who sent letters of congratulations to Stalin on such an event as the twenty-fourth anniversary of the October Revolution or victory over Germany.[7] Not even Stalinist bibliographers bothered to list all these empty documents, and no attempt to fill this gap seems necessary today.

On the other hand, the prewar Stalinist bibliographers and the compilers of the official Sochineniia did pay some attention to the fairly numerous published letters of greetings or congratulations that Stalin addressed (sometimes with a co-signatory) to a variety of notable and humble Soviet citizens, including leading politicians, explorers, successful factory directors, and commanders of military schools.[8] As was noted earlier, an incomplete smattering of documents of this sort did appear in the Sochineniia, and the inclusion of such material in bibliographies treating the post-Sochineniia years implies that it was not to be completely excluded from the final volumes in the series. Since the compilers of the Sochineniia do not make it clear how they distinguished between wheat and chaff, it is impossible to emulate their standard, even if it were desirable to do so. What I have attempted in this listing and in the concurrently prepared supplementary, unofficial volumes of Stalin's Sochineniia[9] is to include only those letters to Soviet citizens that seem to have some content or idea beyond pure formality. This distinction is not always simple, and there is always the possibility

---

[6] E.g., Pravda, April 7, 1944. [7] E.g., Pravda, Nov. 12, 1941.

[8] E.g., Pravda, Jan. 30, 1944.

[9] Stalin, Sochineniia (Stanford, Hoover, 1966), XIV-XVI. These volumes include only Russian language materials and therefore exclude some items presently available only in other languages. But such items (e.g., materials presented in Khrushchev's "secret" speech) are noted in this bibliography.

that some experts in esoteric communication may detect something of interest--if only in the names of the addressees--that would not be noticed by me. One might, for example, ask why Stalin chose to reply in any public form to a few of the hundreds or thousands of known letters from citizens to him and might possibly learn something of interest from a close examination of the identity of the fortunate recipients of replies. Therefore, a listing of the dates of the issues of Pravda in which such seemingly trivial greetings occur is given in a footnote for any reader interested in this arcane topic.[10] The war years are not included here since the Soviet bibliography on this topic (see footnote 3) seems to be complete.

Soviet bibliographers gave exhaustive attention to the military orders that Stalin signed during the war, and there is no doubt that some of these documents are in fact major political speeches. They were published in the Stalin anthology entitled Velikaia Otchestvennaia Voina Sovetskogo Soiuza and would have been included in the sixteenth volume of the Sochineniia, and they deserve inclusion here. On the other hand, many more of these orders bore Stalin's signature only in a purely formal sense and were actually official military communiqués. Only a few really ordered anything except, quite often, the firing of salutes in honor of some victory. Since some scholar might find something of interest in this material regardless of Stalin's personal connection with it, I have a sense of relief in being able to exclude the

---

[10]Greetings or congratulations to Soviet citizens not noted in the main body of the present bibliography appear in the following issues of Pravda after January 1934: 1934--Feb. 27; March 30; April 14; Sept. 17, 22. 1935--Nov. 28, Dec. 30. 1936--Feb. 25; July 17, 22, 24; Aug. 27; Sept. 14, 16, 20; Oct. 10; Nov. 6, 20. 1937--June 21; July 15; Nov. 10. 1938--Feb. 20; June 29; July 3; Oct. 8, 24, 28. 1939-- May 1; Oct. 24. 1940--Jan. 15; Feb. 2; Dec. 19. 1946--Aug. 2; Sept. 18; Oct. 26. 1947--March 5; Aug. 16; Oct. 3, 10, 17; Nov. 4. 1948-- Oct. 16, 25. 1949--Sept. 9; Nov. 20. 1951--April 3. 1952--Jan. 31; April 3.

routine orders from this bibliography, while still referring the peculiar specialist to the reliable Soviet bibliography covering the war (footnote 3) and noting here the issues of Pravda that carry the few postwar formal military orders signed by Stalin.[11]

Quite a different and much scarcer document in which one encounters Stalin's signature is the official eulogy on a deceased Communist leader or the note of condolence to the bereaved. Although most of these writings are not ostensibly very revealing, some scholar may find a useful clue of some sort in this material, even though Stalin's signature is largely a formality and is usually one of many. It therefore seems suitable to provide a list of the dates on which Pravda carried such documents after January 1934, with the name of the deceased following in parentheses.[12]

Still another category of published documents bearing Stalin's signature consists of published letters to foreigners, Communist and non-Communist, mostly dating from the opening of the Second World War. A considerable number of these, addressed to British, French, German, and United States leaders, do contain some substance of great interest. They are, however, available in quite convenient collected form in three widely disseminated books, and to reproduce, in effect, the Stalin entries from the tables of contents of these books would add nothing to scholarly knowledge while greatly lengethening the bibliographical listing in the present volume. It should be enough

---

[11] See Pravda 1946--May 1; July 28; Aug. 18, 25, Sept. 3, 8.

[12] See Pravda 1934--April 11 (Makarovsky); May 12 (M. A. Peshkov--Gorky's son), Dec. 2 (Kirov). 1935--Jan. 26 (Kuibyshev); Aug. 10 (Tovstukha); Sept. 3 (Barbusse). 1936--Feb. 28 (Pavlov); July 16 (Karpinsky). 1937--Feb. 19 (Ordzhonikidze). 1949--July 3 (Dimitrov). It may be noted that after 1937 one had to be somewhat more important to get this type of euology than before that date. The eulogy on Barbusse, which is unlike the others in several respects, is noted in the bibliographical listing here.

to call the reader's attention to the documentary collections in question Other published letters to foreigners, of much less interesting content, are not so readily located. Many are greetings, and nothing more, to the leaders of newly communized states during the years following the Second World War. Since some of these have at least some intellectual content, they have been here included in the main bibliographical listing and in the supplement to the official Sochineniia. Others, which seem to be wholly formal, are simply noted here, [14] along with formal messages to non-Communist foreigners, on the chance that some specialist might find the information useful. This list does not cover the period of the war, which is adequately dealt with by the Soviet bibliography (footnote 3). The date refers to the relevant issue of Pravda except when otherwise noted, and the names in parentheses are the addressees

Finally, there is a category of published documents that does

---

[13] Correspondence between the Chairman of the Council of Ministers of the USSR and the Presidents of the USA and the Prime Ministers of Great Britain during the Great Patriotic War of 1941-1945 (2 vols.; Moscow, Foreign Languages Publishing House, 1957--also available in Russian); Documents on German Foreign Policy, 1918-1945, Series D, Vol. VII (Washington, Government Printing Office, 1949-   ); see also R. Sontag and J. Beddie, eds., Nazi-Soviet Relations 1939-1941 (Washington, Department of State, 1948); Sovetsko-frantsuzskie otnosheniia vo vremia velikoi otechestvennoi voiny 1941-1945 gg. (Moscow, Gos. izd. pol. lit., 1959).

[14] 1936--Oct. 16 (Diaz). 1939--Dec. 25 (various statesmen who sent Stalin birthday greetings--including Hitler). 1947--April 17 (Tito); April 21 (Cyrankiewicz). 1948--April 21 (Cyrankiewicz); June 17 (Gottwald); July 15 (Central Committee of Italian Communist Party); Oct. 13 (Kim Ir Sen*); Dec. 14 (Zapotocki). 1949--April 10 (Dimitrov, Fagerholm); April 21 (Cyrankiewicz); Sept. 23 (Cachin--in For a Lasting Peace...); Oct. 15 (Kim Ir Sen); Dec. 13 (Zapotocki). 1950--May 11 (Grotewohl); Oct. 7 (Grotewohl); Oct. 12 (Kim Ir Sen). 1952--Feb. 14 (Mao Tse-tung); April 19 (Bierut); May 9 (Grotewohl); May 10 (Zapotocki); May 10 (Groza and Gheorghiu-Dej); Aug. 15 (Kim Ir Sen); Aug. 23 (Gheorghiu-Dej); Sept. 9 (Chervenkov); Oct. 1 (Mao Tse-tung); Oct. 7 (Grotewohl). 1953--Feb. 14 (Mao Tse-tung).
*Usually rendered Kim Il Sung in English.

bear Stalin's signature (usually with a co-signatory) and does have major substantive interest, but which nevertheless cannot be considered part of the Stalin literary heritage in any direct sense. These are mainly postanovleniia (resolutions) dealing with a number of major domestic administrative questions between January 1936 and August 1952. Careful students of a number of topics, especially Soviet agriculture, will probably find these documents rewarding and may be interested that these and only these among the published administrative decrees of the Stalin era were emphasized with his signature.[15] This does not imply, however, that he did not stress the importance of various unpublished decrees by signing them, too, as is indicated by several documents in the Smolensk archives.[16]

Having thus eliminated various types of documents that might be included in a list of Stalin's published works after January 1934, the present bibliography is left with only a rather modest list of entries, most of which will be familiar to scholars who have worked in this field. This situation reflects accurately not only the intent of the bibliographer to avoid any pretense of having discovered much of anything within the later Stalin period, but also the intent of Stalin to make almost all of his rare pronouncements stand out as allegedly major additions to Marxist-Leninist literature. Of most of the more important items that appear in this bibliography, it can be said that Stalin saw to it that they were collected and distributed in various anthologies. Such collections, taken together, partly compensate for the absence of

---

[15] See Pravda: 1933--Jan. 1 (included in Part II of this bibliography for continuity). 1936--Jan. 27. 1938--Oct. 8. 1939--May 28; Dec. 20. 1940--April 7, 12, 16, 17. 1940--May 10, 18, 28. 1941--Jan. 12; March 7; June 2, 30; Oct. 19. 1946--Sept. 19. 1949--March 1. 1952--Aug. 20. One other document of this type appears in Bol'shevik, No. 1, 1949, pp. 51-54, but evidently not in Pravda.

[16] Merle Fainsod, Smolensk under Soviet Rule (Cambridge, Harvard University Press, 1958), pp. 80, 81, 185.

Sochineniia volumes. Most of the important documents from February 1934 to the opening of the Second World War were included in the later editions of <u>Voprosy Leninizma</u>, the wartime materials in <u>Velikaia Otchestvennaia Voina Sovetskogo Soiuza</u>, and a number of the postwar statements in the booklets <u>Marksizm i voprosy iazykoznaniia</u> and <u>Ekonomicheskie problemy sotsializma v SSSR</u>.

In closing this introductory essay it is worth noting that there must be a considerable body of unpublished Stalin material, which is beyond the reach of the present investigator. It may well be that an official Stalinist version of volume XIV of the <u>Sochineniia</u> would not have added previously confidential material, for the following list of Stalin's known writings of 1934-1940 is quite large enough to constitute a typical volume in the official series. In any case it seems definite that the Institute of Marxism-Leninism had prepared its version of the Stalin works for this period. On January 12, 1956, <u>Literaturnaia Gazeta</u> noted briefly that volume XIV of the Stalin <u>Sochineniia</u> would soon appear. But the decisive turn against Stalin at the February, 1956, party congress seems to have quashed this publishing venture for the indefinite future--there may even have been some hundreds of thousands of copies in print but suppressed. As for volume XV of the official <u>Sochineniia</u>, it was published in many editions starting in 1938, and there is no doubt as to its contents. That is, this particular volume was scheduled by the editors of the <u>Sochineniia</u> to be the famous <u>Kratkii kurs</u> on party history which had not been wholly attributed to Stalin until 1946. The sixteenth and final intended volume, covering the war years, is much harder to appraise with respect to probable content. The writings and speeches of the leader would not have been enough for an average-sized volume in the series, but the addition of purely formal orders and similar documents bearing his signature could have been used for padding. Certainly fresh, previously unpublished material also could have been used in this volume, although it seems unlikely that this would have included letters to the American and British leaders.

All told, the greatest years in Stalin's career remain extremely ill-documented with materials from his own hand, which implies that the publications listed below are in one sense precious and in another quite inadequate for the study of so complex and consequential a figure.

896.   Letter to Novaia Uda, March 24, 1934.
            P, Mar. 26, 1934.
        XIV, 1.

897.   Letter to the Central Asian Bureau of the Central Committee,
        June 29, 1934.
            Published in Mastera vysokogo urozhaia (Moscow:
        Krest'ianskaia Gazeta, 1936), pp. 324-325, according to
        Kniga i Proletarskaia Revoliutsiia, p. 155. [This item repre-
        sents an exception to the statement in the Introduction that
        "all" documents listed have been found in their original pub-
        lished form.]

898.   O stat'e Engel'sa "Vneshniaia politika russkogo tsarizma."
        [Engels' Article "The Foreign Policy of Russian Tsarism."]
            B, 1941, no. 9, pp. 1-5, signed July 19, 1934.
        XIV, 2-10

899.   Interview with H. G. Wells, July 23, 1934.
            B, 1934, no. 17, pp. 8-18.
        XIV, 11-36.

900.   Zamechaniia po povodu konspekta uchebnika po "Istorii SSSR."
        [Observations Regarding the Synopsis of the Textbook on "The
        History of the USSR."]
            P, Jan. 27, 1936; dated Aug. 8, 1934, signed with Kirov
        and Zhdanov.
        XIV, 37-40.

901.   Zamechaniia o konspekte uchebnika "Novoi istorii." [Observations
        on the Synopsis of the Textbook "Modern History."]
            P, Jan. 27, 1936; dated Aug. 9, 1934, signed with Kirov
        and Zhdanov.
        XIV, 41-45.

902.   Letter to Michurin.
              P, Sept. 23, 1934.
         XIV, Sept. 23, 1934.

903.   Statement at Reception for Metallurgists, Dec. 26, 1934.
              P, Dec. 29, 1934.
         XIV, 47-50.

1935

904.   Letter to the Main Soviet Cinematographic Administration,
         Comrade Shumiatskii.
              P, Jan. 11, 1935.
         XIV, 51-52.

905.   Speech to the Commission for the Drafting of the Model Statute
         for the Rural Artel at the Second Congress of Kolkhoz Shock-
         Workers, Feb. 15, 1935.
              P, Mar. 13, 1935 (excerpts only).
         XIV, 53-54.

906.   Greetings to the First Cavalry Army.
              P, Feb. 24, 1935.
         XIV, 55.

907.   Statement at May Day Reception, May 2, 1935.
              I, May 4, 1936.
         XIV, 56-57.

908.   Speech to Graduating Class of Red Army Academy, May 4, 1935.
              P, May 6, 1935.
         XIV, 58-66.

909.   Speech at Opening Ceremony of the L. M. Kaganovich Metro,
         May 14, 1935.
              P, May 15, 1935.
         XIV, 67-69.

910.   Greetings to the Stalin Special Red-Banner Cavalry Division.
             P, June 18, 1935.
         XIV, 70.

911.   Greetings to Comrade Sokolov.
             P, Aug. 25, 1935.
         XIV, 71.

912.   Letter to Humanité.
             P, Sept. 3, 1935.
         XIV, 72.

913.   Letter to Tsiolkovskii.
             P, Sept. 17, 1935.
         XIV, 73.

914.   Speech at Reception for Women Kolkhoz Shock-Workers of the
         Sugar-Beet Fields by Leaders of the Party and State, Nov. 10,
         1935.
             P, Nov. 11, 1935.
         XIV, 74-77.

915.   Letter to Comrade Egorov.
             P, Nov. 11, 1935.
         XIV, 78.

916.   Speech to the First All-Union Conference of Stakhanovites,
         Nov. 17, 1935.
             P, Nov. 22, 1935.
         XIV, 79-101.

917.   Speech to Conference of the Foremost Combine Operators,
         Dec. 1, 1935.
             P, Dec. 4, 1935.
         XIV, 102-112.

918.   Speech to Conference of Foremost Kolkhoz Workers of
        Tadzhikistan and Turkmenistan with Leaders of the Party and
        State, Dec. 4, 1935.
            P, Dec. 6, 1935.
        XIV, 113-115.

919.   Comment on Maiakovskii.
            P, Dec. 5, 1935. This statement, which appears on p. 4,
        reads "Maiakovskii byl i ostaetsia luchshim, talantlivym
        poetom nashei sovetskoi epokhi. Bezrazlichie k ego pamiati
        i ego proizvedeniiam--prestuplenie." The origin of this com-
        ment does not seem to lie in any known, published work of
        Stalin and was a mystery to the Soviet bibliographers of
        Stalin's day and remains so for the present writer.

                                1936

920.   Interview with Roy Howard, Mar. 1, 1936.
            P, Mar. 5, 1936.
        XIV, 116-131.

921.   Letter to Workers in the Gold Industry.
            P, June 28, 1936.
        XIV, 132.

922.   Speech at Reception for Chkalov, Baidukov, Beliakov.
            P, Aug. 14, 1936.
        XIV, 133-134.

923.   Telegram to Kaganovich, Molotov and other Members of Polit-
        buro, Sept. 25, 1936.
            First revealed in Khrushchev's "secret" speech to the
        Twentieth Party Congress. See B. Wolfe, Khrushchev and
        Stalin's Ghost (London: Atlantic Press, 1957), p. 130.
        Signed with Zhdanov. Original Russian unavailable.

924.   Telegram to Diaz.
            P, Oct. 16, 1936.
        XIV, 135.

925.   O proekte konstitutsii Soiuza SSR. [On the Draft Constitution of
        the USSR.] Nov. 25, 1936.
            P, Nov. 26, 1936.
        XIV, 136-183.

926.   Report of the Editing Commission on the Draft Constitution,
        Dec. 5, 1936.
            P, Dec. 6, 1936.
        XIV, 184-188.

927.   Letter to Largo Caballero, Dec. 31, 1936.
            Signed with Voroshilov, Molotov, published in French in
        The New York Times, June 4, 1939.

                                1937

928.   Letter to Largo Caballero, Feb. 14, 1937.
            Signed with Voroshilov, Molotov, published in The New
        York Times in French, June 4, 1939.

929.   Speeches to the March, 1937, Plenum of the Central Committee.

            O nedostatkakh partiinoi raboty i merakh likvidatsii
        trotsistskikh i inykh dvurushnikov. [On Deficiencies in Party
        Work and Measures for Liquidating Trotskyites and Other
        Double-Dealers.] Mar. 3.
            P, Mar. 29, 1937.
        XIV, 189-224.

            Conclusion, Mar. 5.
            P, Apr. 1, 1937.
        XIV, 225-247.

930.   Letter to the Compilers of the Textbook on the History of the
       All-Union Communist Party (of Bolsheviks).
              P, May 6, 1937.
       XIV, 248-252.

931.   Toast to the Middle and Lower Economic Leaders, Oct. 29,
       1937.
              P, Oct. 31, 1937.
       XIV, 253-255.

932.   Speech to Electors of Stalin Electoral District, Moscow, Dec.
       11, 1937.
              P, Dec. 12, 1937.
       XIV, 256-265.

                              1938

933.   Letter to Comrade Ivan Filipovich Ivanov, Feb. 12, 1938.
              P, Feb. 14, 1938.
       XIV, 266-273.

934.   Letter to Detizdat, Central Committee of Komsomol, Feb. 16,
       1938.
              Published in full in article by P. N. Pospelov, "Piat'desiat
       let Kommunisticheskogi Partii Sovetskogo Soiuza," Voprosy
       Istorii, no. 11, 1953, p. 21.
       XIV, 274.

935.   Speech to Workers of the Higher Schools, May 17, 1938.
              P, May 19, 1938.
       XIV, May 19, 1938.

936.   O dialekticheskom i istoricheskom materializme, Sept., 1938.
       [Dialectical and Historical Materialism.]
              P, Sept. 12, 1938. This essay forms a chapter in the
       famous textbook Istoriia VKP(b). Kratkii kurs, which was
       first published in 1938 as a collective work, and then in 1946
       was attributed to Stalin alone. Later the book was again treate
       as a collective effort, but it appears that the essay cited above
       continues to be regarded as Stalin's work, as it has been from
       the time of its first appearance.
       XIV, 279-326.

936a. Interview with Finskii Vestnik, Dec., 1938.
        Finskii Vestnik, Dec. 16, 1938.

1939

937. Telegram to Oblast and Krai Committee of the Party, Jan. 20,
1939.
        First revealed in Khrushchev's "secret" speech to the
Twentieth Party Congress; published in Wolfe, Khrushchev
and Stalin's Ghost (London: Atlantic Press, 1957), p. 160.
Original Russian unavailable.

938. Speech to the Eighteenth Party Congress, Mar. 10, 1939.
        P, Mar. 11, 1939.
XIV, 327-402.

939. Greetings to First Cavalry Army.
        P, Nov. 19, 1939.
XIV, 403.

940. Letter to the Editor of Pravda. (On the False Communication
of the Havas Agency.)
        P, Nov. 30, 1939.
XIV, 404-405.

1940

941. Thanks for Birthday Greetings.
        P, Feb. 2, 1940.
XIV, 406.

1941

942. Radio Speech, July 3, 1941.
        P, July 3, 1941.
XV, 1-10.

943. Speech to Moscow Soviet, Party and Public Organizations, Nov.
6, 1941.
        P, Nov. 7, 1941.
XV, 11-31.

944.   Speech on Red Square, Nov. 7, 1941.
             P, Nov. 8, 1941.
        XV, 32-35.

                              1942

945.   Order of the Day, no. 55, Feb. 23, 1942.
             P, Feb. 23, 1942.
        XV, 36-44.

946.   Telegram to Komarov, Apr. 12, 1942.
             Iosifu Vissarionovichu Stalinu. Akademiia Nauk SSR
        (Moscow: Izd. Akademii Nauk SSSR, 1949), p. 356.

947.   Order of the Day, no. 130, May 1, 1942.
             P, May 1, 1942.
        XV, 46-56.

948.   Letter to Henry Cassidy, Oct. 3, 1942.
             P, Oct. 5, 1942.
        XV, 57-58.

949.   Speech to Moscow Soviet, Party and Public Organizations,
        Nov. 6, 1942.
             P, Nov. 7, 1942.
        XV, 59-77.

950.   Order of the Day, no. 345, Nov. 7, 1942.
             P, Nov. 7, 1942.
        XV, 78-82.

951.   Letter to Henry Cassidy, Nov. 13, 1942.
             P, Nov. 14, 1942.
        XV, 83-85.

1943

952.   Order of the Day, no. 95, Feb. 23, 1943.
            P, Feb. 23, 1943.
        XV, 86-94.

953.   Order of the Day, no. 195, May 1, 1943.
            P, May 1, 1943.
        XV, 95-102.

954.   Letter to Ralph Parker, May 4, 1943.
            P, May 6, 1943.
        XV, 103.

955.   Letter to Harold King, May 28, 1943.
            P, May 30, 1943.
        XV, 104-105.

956.   Letter to the Presidium of the Union of Polish Patriots in the
        USSR.
            P, June 17, 1943.
        XV, 106.

957.   Speech to Moscow Soviet, Party and Public Organizations,
        Nov. 6, 1943.
            P, Nov. 7, 1943.
        XV, 107-127.

958.   Order of the Day, no. 309, Nov. 7, 1943.
            P, Nov. 7, 1943.
        XV, 128-133.

1944

959.   Order of the Day, no. 16, Feb. 23, 1944.
            P, Feb. 23, 1944.
        XV, 134-142.

960.   Order of the Day, no. 70, May 1, 1944.
            P, May 1, 1944.
        XV, 142-149.

961.   Reply to Pravda Correspondent.
            P, June 14, 1944.
        XV, 150-151.

962.   Speech to Moscow Soviet, Party and Public Organizations,
        Nov. 6, 1944.
            P, Nov. 7, 1944.
        XV, 152-171.

963.   Order of the Day, no. 220, Nov. 7, 1944.
            P, Nov. 7, 1944.
        XV, 172-176.

964.   Speech to Delegation from Warsaw, Nov. 15, 1944.
            P, Nov. 16, 1944.
        XV, 177.

1945

965.   Order of the Day, no. 5, Feb. 23, 1945.
            P, Feb. 23, 1945.
        XV, 178-182.

966.   Letter to P. Groza and G. Tatarescu, Mar. 9, 1945.
            P, Mar. 10, 1945.
        XV, 183.

967.   Speech on the Signing of the Mutual Aid Treaty with Poland,
        Apr. 21, 1945.
                P, Apr. 22, 1945.
        XV, 184-187.

968.   Radio Speech, Apr. 28, 1945.
                P, Apr. 28, 1945.
        XV, 188.

969.   Order of the Day, no. 20, 1945.
                P, May 1, 1945.
        XV, 189-194.

970.   Order of the Day, no. 369, May 9, 1945.
                P, May 10, 1945.
        XV, 195-196.

971.   Radio Speech, May 9, 1945.
                P, May 10, 1945.
        XV, 197-199.

972.   Letter to Ralph Parker, May 18, 1945.
                P, May 19, 1945.
        XV, 200-201.

973.   Letter to the Editors of Komsomol'skaia Pravda.
                P, May 24, 1945.
        XV, 202.

974.   Toasts at Reception for Red Army Commanders, May 24, 1945.
                P, May 25, 1945.
        XV, 203-204.

975.   Letter to Pionerskaia Pravda.
                P, June 10, 1945.
        XV, 205.

976.   Statement at Reception for Participants in Victory Parade,
       June 25, 1945.
            P, June 27, 1945.
       XV, 206.

977.   Order of the Day, no. 371, July 22, 1945.
            P, July 22, 1945.
       XV, 207-208.

978.   Letter to Tsian Chzhun-chzhen, Aug. 18, 1945.
            P, Aug. 19, 1945.
       XV, Aug. 19, 1945.

979.   Letter to Choibalsan.
            P, Aug. 29, 1945.
       XV, 210.

980.   Letter to Tsian Chzhun-chzhen.
            P, Aug. 31, 1945.
       XV, 211.

981.   Address to "The People," Sept. 2, 1945.
            P, Sept. 3, 1945.
       XV, 212-216.

982.   Order of the Day, no. 373, Sept. 3, 1945.
            P, Sept. 5, 1945.
       XV, 217-218.

                          1946

983.   Author's Preface to Sochineniia, Jan. 1946.
            Sochineniia, I, xi-xv.

984.   Speech to Electors of the Stalin Electoral District of Moscow,
       Feb. 9, 1946.
            P, Feb. 10, 1946.
       XVI, 1-22.

985.   Order of the Day, no. 8, Feb. 23, 1946.
          P, Feb. 23, 1946.
        XVI, 23-28.

986.   Letter to Razin, Feb. 23, 1946.
          B, 1947, no. 3, pp. 6-8.
        XVI, 29-34.

987.   Interview with Pravda Correspondent, March 13, 1946.
          P, Mar. 14, 1946.
        XVI, 35-43.

988.   Message to Supreme Soviet, Mar. 15, 1946.
            Zasedaniia Verkhovnogo Soveta SSSR (Pervaia sessiia).
        Stenograficheskii otchet (Moscow: izd. Verkhovnogo Soveta
        SSSR, 1946), p. 82.

989.   Letter to Eddy Gilmore, Mar. 22, 1946.
          P, Mar. 23, 1946.
        XVI, 45-46.

990.   Letter to Hugh Bailey, Mar. 25, 1946.
          P, Mar. 27, 1946.
        XVI, 47.

991.   Order of the Day, no. 7, May 1, 1946.
          P, May 1, 1946.
        XVI, 48-52.

992.   Letter to Alexander Werth.
          I, Sept. 24, 1946. Undated; it is in reply to an inquiry
        received Sept. 17.
        XVI, 53-56.

993.   Letter to Hugh Bailey.
          P, Oct. 30, 1946. Undated; it is in reply to any inquiry
        received Oct. 23.
        XVI, 57-63.

994.   Greetings to Pan-Slav Congress, Dec. 8, 1946.
           Slaviane, no. 1, 1947, p. 17.
       XVI, 64.

                        1947

995.   Interview with Elliot Roosevelt, Dec. 21, 1946.
           P, Jan. 23, 1947.
       XVI, 65-70.

996.   Order of the Day, no. 10, Feb. 23, 1947.
           P, Feb. 23, 1947.
       XVI, 71-74.

997.   Interview with Harold Stassen, Apr. 9, 1947.
           P, May 8, 1947.
       XVI, 75-92.

998.   Greetings to the City of Moscow.
           P, Sept. 7, 1947.
       XVI, 93-96.

                        1948

999.   Letter to Paasiviki, Feb. 22, 1948.
           I, Feb. 29, 1948.
       XVI, 97-98.

1000. Speech at Reception for Finnish Delegation, Apr. 7, 1948.
           P, Apr. 13, 1948.
       XVI, 99-101.

1001. Letter to Henry Wallace, May 17, 1948.
           P, May 18, 1948.
       XVI, 102-104.

1002.   Interview with Pravda Correspondent, Oct. 28, 1948.
              P, Oct. 29, 1948.
         XVI, 105-107.

                              1949

1003.   Letter to Kingsbury Smith, Jan. 30, 1949.
              P, Jan. 31, 1949.
         XVI, 108-109.

1004.   Letter to Wilhelm Pieck and Otto Grotewohl, Oct. 13, 1949.
              P, Oct. 14, 1949.
         XVI, 110-111.

                              1950

1005.   Letter to Maurice Thorez.
              P, Apr. 28, 1950.
         XVI, 112.

1006.   Letter to the Central Council of the Union of Free German
         Youth.
              P, June 2, 1950.
         XVI, 113

1007.   Marksizm i voprosy iazykoznaniia [Marxism and Problems of
         Linguistics]
              Consisting of:
         Otnositel'no marksizma v iazykoznanii [Concerning Marxism
         in Linguistics].
              P, June 20, 1950.
         XVI, 117-148.

         K nekotorym voprosam iazykoznaniia--otvet tovarishchu E.
         Krasheninnikovoi [On Certain Problems of Linguistics--Reply
         to Comrade E. Krasheninnikova]. June 29, 1950.
              P, July 4, 1950.
         XVI, 149-157.
(continued on next page)

1007 (continued).

> Otvet tovarishcham [Reply to Comrades].
> Tovarishchu Sanzheevu [To Comrade Sanzheev]. July 11, 1950.
>> P, Aug. 2, 1950.
> XVI, 158-159

> Tovarishcham D. Belkinu i S. Fureru [To Comrades D. Belkin
> and S. Furer]. July 22, 1950.
>> P, Aug. 2, 1950.
> XVI, 160-162.

> Tovarishchu A. Kholopovu [To Comrade A. Kholopov]. July 28,
> 1950.
>> P, Aug. 2, 1950.
> XVI, 163-171.

1008.   Letter to Nehru, July 15, 1950.
>> P, July 18, 1950.
> XVI, 172.

1951

1009.   Interview with Pravda Correspondent, Feb. 16, 1951.
>> P, Feb. 17, 1951.
> XVI, 173-180.

1010.   Letter to Mao Tse-tung, Sept. 2, 1951.
>> P, Sept. 3, 1951.
> XVI, 181-182.

1011.   Interview with Pravda Correspondent.
>> P, Oct. 6, 1951.
> XVI, 183-185.

1012.   Letter to Kiisi Ivamoto, Dec. 31, 1951.
>> P, Jan. 1, 1952.
> XVI, 186-187.

1952

1013. Ekonomicheskie problemy sotsializma v SSSR [Economic Problems of Socialism in the USSR]
Consisting of:
Uchastnikam ekonomicheskoi diskussii. Zamechaniia po ekono-
micheskim voprosam, sviazannym c noiabr'skoi diskussiei
1951 goda [To Participants in the Economic Discussion. Remarks on Economic Questions Connected with the November
1951 Discussion]. Signed Feb. 1, 1952.
P, Oct. 3, 4, 1952.
XVI, 188-245.

Otvet tovarishchu Notkinu, Aleksandru Il'ichu [Reply to Com-
rade Notkin, Alexander Ilich]. Apr. 21, 1952.
P, Oct. 3, 1952.
XVI, 146-257.

Ob oshibkakh Tovarishcha Iaroshenko, L.D. [Concerning the
Errors of Comrade Iaroshenko, L.D.] May 22, 1952.
P, Oct. 4, 1952.
XVI, 258-290.

Otvet Tovarishcham Saninoi, A.V., and Venzheru, V.G.
[Reply to Comrades Sanina, A.V., and Venzher, V.G.].
Sept. 28, 1952.
P, Oct. 4, 1952.
XVI, 291-304.

1014. Letter to American Newspaper Editors.
P, Apr. 2, 1952.
XVI, 305-306.

1015. Greeting to Pioneers.
P, May 20, 1952.
XVI, 307.

1016. Letter to Mao Tse-tung, Sept. 2, 1952.
P, Sept. 3, 1952.
XVI, 308-309.

1017.   Speech to Nineteenth Party Congress, Oct. 14, 1952.
          P, Oct. 15, 1952.
     XVI, 310-315.

1018.   Letter to James Reston.
          P, Dec. 26, 1952.
     XVI, 316.

APPENDIX A
(See entries 227 and 253)

NOTE ON STALIN'S STATEMENTS IN THE CENTRAL COMMITTEE,
AUGUST 1917 - FEBRUARY 1918

Although the Khrushchev regime published minutes of a number
of its Central Committee meetings, full accounts of what was said in
earlier meetings of this body are exceptional, and we have official versions of Stalin's statements to the Central Committee only as extracts
in most cases. In 1927, however, the party historical journal,
Proletarskaia Revoliutsiia, published a version of the minutes of the
Central Committee covering part of the period August, 1917 - February,
1918,[1] and this was republished and presumably improved as a book in
1929.[2] Then, in 1958, a new, revised edition of the same body of
material was published,[3] utilizing additional materials to piece
together what must be a somewhat informal record in any case, owing
to the conditions in which the committee met in 1917. One may
wonder whether or not this is the fullest account that Soviet editors
might give of these meetings, for Trotsky alleged that Stalin

---

[1] Proletarskaia Revoliutsiia, 1927, nos. 8-9, pp. 321-351; no.
10, pp. 246-298; no. 11, pp. 202-214; no. 2, pp. 132-169.

[2] Protokoly tsentral'nogo komiteta RSDRP(b) Avgust 1917--fevral'
1918 (Moscow: Gosizdat, 1929). This book has not been available to the
present writer; however, it is supposed to cover the entire period August,
1917--Febrary, 1918, while the journal Proletarskaia Revoliutsiia
omitted a period at the end of 1917 and beginning of 1918.

[3] Protokoly tsentral'nogo komiteta RSDRP(b) avgust 1917--fevral'
1918 (Moscow: Gos. izd. pol. lit., 1958).

doctored the records of these meetings prior to their first publication (but the post-Stalin version does not appear to revise anything in an anti-Stalin direction). There does, however, seem to be something inhibiting post-Stalin historical editors in connection with the Central Committee archives, for in 1957 Voprosy Istorii (no. 2, p. 198) referre to the planned publication in connection with the 40th anniversary of the October Revolution of a volume entitled Protokoly tsentral'nogo komite RSDRP(b) covering March, 1917 – April, 1918. Since this would have dealt with the early period of the Revolution, in which Stalin was a "compromiser," it appears likely that the planned volume would have included some material harmful to his image as a staunch Leninist. Quite possibly this intended publication was part of the revision of party history to the detriment of Stalin in which the journal Voprosy Istorii, and especially E. N. Burdzhalov of its editorial board, played such a considerable role until a number of editors were purged in April, 1957, only shortly after the announcement of the planned publication of the extended Protokoly. In any case, we are still awaiting this book.

What we do have concerning Stalin's own statements in the Centr Committee between August, 1917, and February, 1918, is therefore a record that is not above question. With this warning, however, it may at least be useful to provide the researcher with a somewhat more thorough list of Stalin's published statements in the Central Committee that appears in his Sochineniia. In this official collection the editors have chosen to republish two of his statements of 1917-1918, while excluding a number of others that may be of interest to some researche Therefore, the following list summarizes Stalin's statements to the Central Committee as listed in the 1958 edition of the Protokoly:

Date of Statement   Location in "Protokoly" (1958 ed.)

Aug. 16, 1917 .... p. 24

Sept. 15, 1917 .... p. 55

Oct. 5, 1917 .... p. 76

Oct. 16, 1917 .... p. 100 [In S; see entry 217.]

Oct. 20, 1917 .... pp. 106-108

Oct. 21, 1917 .... p. 118

Nov. 29, 1917 .... p. 150

Jan. 11, 1918 .... p. 171 [In S; see entry 243.]

Jan. 19, 1918 .... p. 178

Jan. 24, 1918 .... p. 193

Feb. 18, 1918 [NS] .... pp. 200, 202

Feb. 23, 1918 [NS] .... pp. 212-213, 217

Oktiabr'skii perevorot i natsional'nyi vopros

ОКТЯБРЬСКИЙ ПЕРЕВОРОТ И НАЦИОНАЛЬНЫЙ ВОПРОС

Национальный вопрос не есть нечто самодовлеющее, раз навсегда данное. Являясь лишь частью общего вопроса о преобразовании существующего строя, национальный вопрос целиком определяется условиями социальной обстановки, характером власти в стране и, вообще, всем ходом общественного развития. Это особенно заметно в революционные эпохи, когда национальный вопрос и национальное движение быстро и на глазах у всех меняют свое содержание в зависимости от хода и исхода революции.

В эпоху буржуазной революции (февраль 1917 г.) национальное движение носило характер буржуазно-освободительного движения. Национальные «советы», национальные «парламенты», национальные «учредительные собрания», покрывшие тогда окраины России — вот те институты, вокруг которых собирала силы национальная буржуазия. Речь шла тогда об освобождении от царизма, как «основной» причины национального гнета, и образовании национальных буржуазных государств в роде тех, которые создались в Европе в середине XIX века, в эпоху т. н. «национальных войн», в эпоху начального периода капитализма. Право наций на самоопределение толковалось, как право на образование национального буржуазного государства. При этом упускалось из виду, что на смену царизму идет оголенный, лишенный маски, империализм, что он, этот империализм, является более сильным и более опасным врагом национальностей, основой нового национального гнета.

Уничтожение царизма и появление у власти буржуазии не повело, однако, к уничтожению национального гнета. Старая грубая форма национального гнета сменилась новой утонченной, но зато более опасной формой гнета. Занявшая место царизма буржуазия, империалистская по своей природе, не только не отказалась от угнетения трудовых масс национальностей России, но призвала население к продолжению войны для подчинения новых земель, новых колоний и национальностей. К этому толкала ее не только внутренная природа империализма, но и наличие на Западе старых империалистических государств, неудержимо стремившихся к подчинению новых земель и национальностей и угрожавших ей сужением сферы ея влияния. Борьба империалистических государств за подчинение мелких национальностей, как условие существования этих государств, — вот какая картина раскрылась в ходе империалисткой войны.

Таким образом старое буржуазно-демократическое толкование принципа самоопределения с течением времени превратилось в фикцию, лишилось своего революционного смысла. Ибо при условиях воинствующего империализма не могло быть и речи о независимости мелких государств. «Получившая» «независимость», например, Норвегия (в 1905 г.) на деле попала в самую реальную зависимость от одного из старых империалистических государств. «Добившаяся» на-днях «независимости» Чехия на деле является сугубо зависимой от международного империализма. Становится ясным, что освобождение угнетенных национальностей немыслимо без разрыва с империализмом, низвержения «своей» буржуазии и взятия власти самими трудовыми массами.

Это особенно ярко сказалось после октябрьского переворота. Решительно порвав с империализмом старых государств и передав власть трудовым массам национальностей России, октябрьский переворот одним взмахом поставил национальный вопрос на должную, **революционную** почву. Только теперь почувствовали себя рабочие и крестьяне национальностей России свободными, независимыми и, получив свободу, поспешили использовать свое право на самоопределение или установления свободного федеративного союза народов России. Только теперь стало очевидным, что буржуазия национальностей России стремилась не к действительному освобождению от национального гнета, а лишь к свободе выколачивания барышей: в то время, как, например, финские рабочие боролись за независимость своего социалистического отечества от империализма, финская буржуазия приглашала в свою страну иноземных империалистов; в то время, как украинские рабочие проливали кровь за свободу советской Украины, украинская буржуазия заключала союз с империалистическими угнетателями. Старое **буржуазное** понимание принципа самоопределения и «защиты отечества» столкнулось с новым **социалистическим** пониманием во всей своей конкретности.

Так, октябрьский переворот, покончив с старым буржуазным национальным движением, открыл эру нового социалистического движения трудовых масс угнетенных национальностей, направленного против всякого национального гнета, против власти буржуазии и империализма.

Смертный грех II-го Интернационала и его главы Каутского в том, между прочим, и состоит, что они все время сбивались на буржуазное понимание принципа самоопределения, не понимали революционного значения последнего и не умели или не хотели ставить национальный вопрос на революционную почву открытой борьбы с империализмом.

Тупость социал-демократов Австрии типа Бауэра и Реннера в том, собственно, и состоит, что они не поняли неразрывной связи национального вопроса с вопросом о власти, стараясь отделить национальный вопрос от политики и замкнуть его в рамки культурно-просветительных вопросов, при чем, разумеется, никакого разрешения национального вопроса из этого не получилось.

Некоторые товарищи думают, что принцип самоопределения и «защиты отечества», а буржуазное их толкование тий в обстановке подымающей ся социалистической революции. Но это неверно. Отменены не самоопределение и «защита отечества», а буржуазное их толкование. Достаточно взглянуть на оккупированные области, изнывающие под гнетом империализма, и рвущиеся к освобождению, достаточно взглянуть на Россию, ведущую ныне революционную войну в интересах защиты социалистического отечества от хищников мирового империализма, достаточно вдуматься в разыгрывающиеся теперь события в Австро-Венгрии, достаточно взглянуть на порабощенные колонии и полуколонии, с надеждою смотрящие на Россию и уже организующие у себя советы депутатов (Индия—Китай!), — достаточно взглянуть на все это, чтобы понять все революционное значение принципа самоопределения в его социалистическом толковании.

Великое мировое значение октябрьского переворота в России в том, между прочим, и состоит, что он открыл широкие возможности, открыл действительные пути для действительного освобождения угнетенных народов и колоний от ига империализма, от когтей национального гнета.

Этим, собственно, и об'ясняется тот неописуемый энтузиазм, с которым относятся ныне к российскому пролетариату угнетенные народы Востока и Запада.

Этим, главным образом, и об'ясняется то зверское бешенство, с которым набросились ныне на Советскую Россию империалистические хищники всего мира.

И. Сталин

APPENDIX C
(See entry 662)

The Russian material reproduced below is the opening portion of the predislovie to the Stalin anthology Na putiakh k oktiabr'iu (Moscow, 1925). The latter portions of this predislovie do appear in Stalin's Sochineniia, part as a note to the article "Protiv federalizma" (entry 141) and part of the article "Oktiabr'skaia revoliutsiia i tatika russkikh kommunistov" (entry 662). However, the following material was entirely omitted from the Sochineniia (ellipsis five lines before end is in original edition):

ПРЕДИСЛОВИЕ

Настоящая книжка представляет сборник статей и речей автора за март—октябрь 1917 года. В сборник попало все сколько-нибудь важное и сохранившееся. Не попали лишь злободневные заметки и мелкие статейки автора из отделов «Отклики» и «Обзор печати» в «Правде», «Рабочем Пути» и т. д. за август—октябрь 1917 г., так как мне казалось, что они, увеличив объем книжки, не дали бы, между тем, читателю чего-либо нового в сравнении с основными статьями. Должен сказать, что я долго не решался издать даже основные статьи предоктябрьского периода, ибо для меня было ясно, что они не могут представить для читателя и сотой доли того интереса, какой представляет, например, XIV том сочинений Ленина. И, вообще, стоит ли заниматься изданием статей и речей отдельных авторов после того, как партия получила от Ленина такое наследство, как XIV том его сочинений? И если я все же решился издать теперь этот сборник, то это потому, что за последнее время интерес к Октябрю, особенно в связи с последней дискуссией, возрос среди членов партии неимоверно. Я думаю, что для товарищей, желающих изучить Октябрьскую революцию, настоящий сборник мог бы представить не бесполезный м а т е - р и а л .

Весь материал сборника собран товарищем Товстухой, без помощи которого сборник не мог бы вообще выйти в свет. Издается этот материал, конечно, без изменений, если не считать некоторых стилистических поправок, внесенных в «политический отчет» на июльской общегородской конференции Ленинградской организации и на VI съезде партии, ранее автором непросмотренный. Этим, собственно, и объясняется, что дело издания сборника обошлось без особой для этого предмета редакции.

Два необходимых замечания.

Первое замечание касается первых трех статей в сборнике. Эти статьи отражают известные колебания большинства нашей партии по вопросам о мире и власти Советов, имевшие место, как известно, в марте—апреле 1917 года. Это был период крутой ломки старых позиций. Старая платформа прямого свержения правительства теперь уже не отвечала действительности. Теперь уже нельзя было итти на немедленное свержение правительства, связанного с Советами, ибо кто хотел свергнуть тогда Временное Правительство, тот должен был свергнуть и Советы. Но нельзя было также вести политику поддержки

Временного Правительства, ибо это правительство являлось правительством империализма. Нужна была новая ориентировка партии. Немудрено, что большевики, разбросанные царизмом по тюрьмам и ссылкам и теперь только получившие возможность съехаться с разных концов России для выработки новой платформы, — не смогли в один присест разобраться в новом положении. Не мудрено, что в поисках новой ориентировки партия остановилась тогда на полдороге в вопросах о мире и о власти Советов. Понадобились знаменитые «апрельские тезисы» Ленина для того, чтобы партия смогла одним взмахом выйти на новую дорогу. Я уже говорил раз в своей речи на фракции В.Ц.С.П.С., что эту ошибочную позицию я разделял тогда с большинством партии и отказался от нее полностью в середине апреля, присоединившись к «апрельским тезисам» Ленина ...

Второе замечание касается статьи «Против федерализма» (см. стр. 12). Статья эта выражает господствовавшее тогда в партии отрицательное отношение к федеративному устройству государства.

INDEX

INDEX

This index was prepared by the staff of the Hoover Institution on the basis of the headings or titles of entries in this bibliography. An excellent index covering the substance as well as the titles of works by Stalin that were included in the official Sochineniia is: Matlock, Jack F., Jr., assisted by Holling, Fred C. Jr., Index to J. V. Stalin's Works (Russian Edition) (Washington, Department of State, 1955).

Letters to: